ULURU

ULURU

An Aboriginal history of Ayers Rock

ROBERT LAYTON

Australian Institute of Aboriginal Studies
Canberra 1986

Published in Australia by the
Australian Institute of Aboriginal Studies
GPO Box 553, Canberra, ACT 2601.

The views expressed in this publication are those of the author
and not necessarily those of the Australian Institute
of Aboriginal Studies.

The Australian Institute of Aboriginal Studies is grateful for the
generous assistance of the Department of Aboriginal Affairs in the
publication of this book.

National Library of Australia
Cataloguing in Publication data:

   Layton, Robert, 1944-
     Uluru.

    Bibliography.
    Includes index.
    ISBN 0 85575 161 4.

    [1]. Aborigines, Australian—Australia, Central—Culture.
    [2]. Aborigines, Australian—Australia, Central—Land tenure.
    [3]. Pitjantjatjara (Australian people). [4]. Yankunytjatjara
    (Australian people). I. Australian Institute of Aboriginal
    Studies. II. Title.

   305.8'9915'0994291

Typeset by Adelaide Phototype Bureau.
Printed in Australia by Brown Prior Anderson Pty Ltd, Melbourne.

ERRATA

In the production of the book a number of captions became inadvertently attached to the wrong pictures. We apologise for any inconvenience to our readers. The captions on pages 7, 10 and 11 (left) belong on pages 11 (left), 7 and 10. The captions on pages 20 and 21 (left) have been interchanged as have those on pages 27 (left) and 28.

CONTENTS

My thanks go primarily to the senior Aboriginal men who spent long hours with me explaining aspects of their culture and taking me to sites. Paddy Uluru, Nipper Winmati, Pompy Wanampi, Pompy Douglas, Toby Nangina, Bill Ukai, Peter Bulla, Stanley Kumintjara, Tjuki and Charlie Wiliyati were especially helpful. During our stay at Ayers Rock, we received a great deal of assistance and hospitality from the resident staff of the Northern Territory Parks and Wildlife Service, particularly Derek Roff, Stan Cawood, Denis and Alison Matthews, and Trevor, Wendy and Dusty Shelverton. Chris Marshall and Neville Jones of the Department of Aboriginal Affairs were generous with advice and hospitality. Many of the bush trips made to locate and learn about sites were carried out jointly with the Reverend Bill Edwards, who was the Uniting Church Minister at Amata and is a former Superintendent of Ernabella Community. I am especially grateful for the amount of time he was able to spare to make these joint expeditions and his help in collecting and understanding the material obtained on them. Ken Liberman accompanied me on a trip in the Petermann Ranges and helped with work at Docker River.

Much of the material contained in Chapters 1 to 5 is taken from the Ayers Rock Claim Book

(Layton & Rowell 1979). Meredith Rowell helped collect and present historical and genealogical material; Chapters 4 and 5 draw in part on her contributions. I would like to acknowledge the stimulus received from working with the Central Land Council during the claim, particularly in discussions of the material on land tenure with Rod Hagen, Dan Vachon, Geoff Eames and Ross Howie. Both Dan Vachon and Noel Wallace, who was helpful in both discussion and correspondence, have been generous in passing on the results of their own research.

The system of references in this book is complicated by the need to refer to a variety of material. References of the form—SG52-12 388754—are to topographic maps of the 1:250 000 series with non-metric grid. References in the series AA1 to AA21 are to material in the Australian archives, and those in the series WB1 to WB5 are Welfare Branch reports. The full references to these two series are given on pp.133-4. References of the form—transcript pp.783-4—are to the transcript of evidence for the Ayers Rock land claim. Most plant species are referred to in the text only by their common European names or Aboriginal names—scientific names are given in Appendix C.

In 1973, the Federal Government's Standing Committee on Environment and Conservation recommended that the traditional rights of Aboriginal people associated with the area of the Ayers Rock-Mount Olga National Park should be protected and that these people should play a central role in the management of the Park. As a result, the Northern Territory Reserves Board, which then administered the area, sought identification of the correct Aboriginal people. Although the names of some important men were soon obtained, subsequent investigation showed that the pattern of traditional rights was a complex one. Later, in 1976, Aboriginal men associated with Ayers Rock and the Olgas told the Department of Aboriginal Affairs that they wanted a researcher to record local traditions. The Department then wrote to Dr Peter Ucko, Principal of the Australian Institute of Aboriginal Studies (where I was working as a research anthropologist), asking the Institute to provide someone to carry out research into local traditions and rights to land. The letter pointed out that the Central Land Council had lodged a land claim on country adjacent to the National Park and would also require a researcher to help document the claim, suggesting the same person might also do this. The research that followed forms the basis of this book.

Much of the material was collected in the field during three periods my wife and I spent at Ayers Rock: September to December 1977, March to July 1978 and February to April 1979. Further material is taken from the evidence presented during the hearing of the land claim in April and May of 1979.

The book is divided into three parts, the first of which deals with those aspects of Aboriginal life that were established before the arrival of European settlers, including religion, subsistence and land ownership. Much of the material presented in Part One describes a living culture and was collected by living with men and women in the region. Contemporary information was supplemented by people's own accounts of how their lives had been different before contact. Part Two describes how Aboriginal life was changed by contact with White people, looking first at the history of contact largely from the White perspective, then at the Aboriginal response. Finally, Part Three outlines the Aboriginal Land Rights Act in the Northern Territory and analyses the land claim made at Ayers Rock under this Act.

PART ONE

Traditions

CHAPTER 1

The tjukurrpa

Aboriginal culture has its roots in the *tjukurrpa*, or Dreamtime, when groups of ancestral beings crossed the landscape, leaving their mark in the form of hills, creeks, caves and other topographic features. The ancestors' adventures are recorded in rituals and epic song cycles, called *inma*, and their rich detail is summarised and commented on in stories or myths. The events chronicled in the songs and stories established the rules of Aboriginal social life as well as explaining how the landscape came to be. The creation of Uluru (Ayers Rock) and its features are described in several stories. The accounts which follow are built up from episodes told on many occasions.

On 10 December 1977 I was taken to see a hill called Wiputa, associated with the legend of the Two Boys who built Uluru from mud during the *tjukurrpa*. By then we had been living at Uluru for three months, and were staying at Amata for a few days, as guests of the Uniting Church Minister Bill Edwards and his wife Val. Paddy Uluru and his son Albie travelled down with us, and met with Paddy's two old friends Pompy Douglas and Pompy Wanampi, who live at Amata. According to Aboriginal custom the two Pompys are the living re-embodiment of the boys of the legend. As we drove east along the old road between Amata and Mulga Park a perenti—a large lizard—stepped out of the dry grass ahead of us. I braked to avoid it, but the perenti swung round in a shower of dust and raced away over the scrub. Paddy urged me to follow, so we swung off the track and bounced furiously along for quarter of a mile, taking a line slightly to one side of the fleeing reptile until eventually it crawled under a pile of brushwood. Then Pompy Wanampi took his .22 rifle and walked over to a point some 3 metres from the victim. The old men still approach an animal as close as they would have done when using spears. Albie urged him to shoot from further away, telling me later he'd heard that perentis may attack those who go too close. But Pompy didn't miss, and when Albie picked up the dead animal it measured about 2 metres from nose to tail. Pompy carefully broke each leg, explaining that even after death the perenti's fearsome claws might embed themselves in someone's arm or leg as the muscles contract.

We proceeded in a cheerful mood to Wiputa where the Toyota was parked and we approached the low hill. Just to the south is a sand dune which was a traditional Aboriginal camp. It was here Pompy Douglas was born some seventy years previously. Wiputa is a dome of orange rock on which grow scattered trees. On its south-east side is the course of a small dry creek. A creamy coloured area of rock to one side of the creek marks the point where the Two Boys camped during the creation period. From this camp they went hunting among the low hills further south and speared a euro wallaby. A rock hole in the dry creek bed is the remains of their ground oven,

where they lit a fire and buried the euro to cook it. As it cooked, the tail of the euro cracked, and the boys tossed it behind them where it fell on top of the hill.

As we toiled up the side of the hill, I was reminded that this was summer a few miles south of the tropics when I noticed my midday shadow on the rock beneath my feet; it consisted of two stubby arms emerging from the shadow of my hat. Pompy Douglas was striding on, and I scurried behind him while he continued to recount the legends of the surrounding hills. As we climbed, we could see spirals of dust rising from the mulga flats to the north, as willy-willies ran over the hot plains. At the top we found Paddy Uluru already waiting for us, sitting under a lone tree next to the principal feature of the hill, a long crack in its smooth surface about 1 metre wide and up to 6 metres deep. Some boulders had fallen inside. This is the very euro tail itself, split where it fell when discarded by the two boys. Paddy and Pompy explained how Aboriginal children used to climb down into the crack at the shallow end and dance at the bottom, making dust rise into the open air. This they did when their parents were camped at Pompy's birth place.

For all the old men's energy there was now a general feeling that we needed a cool drink, so we drove on to Mulga Park homestead, whose owner runs a store for the local Aboriginal community.

To our disappointment they were out of cool drinks, but Pompy Wanampi and Albie bought everyone a tin of pineapple segments. We punctured the lids to drink the sugary juice, then drove westward again as far as the foot of a hill associated with another of Uluru's legends; the epic of the Mala Wallaby Men. The Mala were chased from Uluru by a devil dingo sent to kill them by their enemies at Kikingkura (Docker River). While the perenti cooked in a ground oven, dug in sandy soil, the old men talked about how the Mala had fled from Uluru, pursued by the malevolent dog. We climbed the hill to see the rock shelter where the Mala camped during their flight, and the men sang verses of the traditional song cycle describing this portion of the Mala Men's journey. Inside the rock shelter there were paintings, but Paddy Uluru declined to explain these to me and seemed, in a discreet gesture, to restrain Pompy Douglas from explaining them also. It was to be some months before Paddy was willing to talk about sacred paintings.

This day was typical of many, when the men with whom I worked, patiently taught me their traditions. Legends are not told in their full form at once; incidents are related when an occasion arises to visit the appropriate place and gradually more profound aspects of the narrative are revealed to give a deeper understanding of why the legends play so central a part in Aboriginal life within the region.

The Wiyai Kutjara story (The Two Boys)

Uluru (Ayers Rock itself) was built up during the creation period by the two boys who played in the mud after rain. When they had finished their game they travelled south to Wiputa, on the northern side of the Musgrave Ranges, where they killed and cooked the euro. Then the boys turned north again toward Atila (Mount Conner). A few miles south-west of the Mount, at Anari one boy threw his *tjuni* (wooden club) at a hare wallaby, but the club struck the ground and made a fresh-water spring. This boy refused to reveal where he had found the water and the other boy nearly died of thirst. Fighting together, the two boys made their way to the table-topped Mount Conner, on top of which their bodies are preserved as boulders.

The Mala story (The Hare Wallabies)

The Mala wallabies came from Mawurungu, near Yuendumu, travelling south through the Haasts Bluff area and arriving at Uluru on its northern side at Katjitilkil. Here, they began to dance, the men at one site, the women at another. When the women were not dancing, they gathered food for the whole group. The women's camp was at Taputji, the small isolated dome on the north-east side of Uluru, where one of their *wana* (digging sticks) can be seen transformed into stone.

While the dances were in progress, the Mala received an invitation to go to Kikingkura, near

The *wana* (digging stick) transformed into stone at Taputji

Docker River, to attend the dances of the Wintalka men. The men sent their invitation through Panpanpanala, the Bell-Bird. But the Mala were already committed to their own celebrations, so they refused to leave, and the Bell-Bird returned to the Wintalka in the Petermann Ranges calling 'Pak, Pak' ('They can't come, they can't come'), the call he makes today.

When they heard that their invitation had been rejected, the Wintalka men decided to send a malevolent dingo-like *mamu* (an evil spirit) to punish the Mala. This creature, called Kurrpanngu, ran eastwards until he had picked up the Mala track at Mulyayiti (Mount Currie), then turned south and followed them to Uluru. He crept up to Tjukutjapinya, where the Mala women were dancing. The hair skirts, or *mawulari*, worn by the women were transformed into pendant cones of rock at Tjukutjapi rockshelter. Kurrpanngu peered over a projecting rock spur, but the women drove him off, and he continued around the base of the Rock to Inintitjara, where the Mala men were sleeping. Lunpa, the Kingfisher woman, was with them, and she called out a warning but was too late to prevent Kurrpanngu leaping into the camp. At Inintjitjara, Lunpa is transformed into a boulder, looking up at the paw marks Kurrpanngu left in the side of the cliff.

The surviving Mala ran southwards from Uluru, splitting into two lines. One line ran close to the northern spur of the Musgrave Ranges on to

Ulkiya, the other fled past Altjinta, near the present site of Mulga Park Homestead.

The Kuniya story (The Pythons)

The Kuniya converged on Uluru from three directions. One group came westward from Waltanta (the present site of Erldunda homestead), and Paku-paku; another came south through Wilpiya (Wilbia Well); and a third, northwards, from the area of Yunanpa (Mitchell's Knob). One of the Kuniya women carried her eggs on her head, using a *manguri* (grass head-pad) to cushion them. She buried these eggs at the eastern end of Uluru. While they were camped at Uluru, the Kuniya were attacked by a party of Liru (poisonous snake) warriors. The Liru had journeyed along the southern flank of the Petermann Ranges from beyond Wangkari (Gills Pinnacle).

At Alyurungu, on the south-west face of Uluru, are pock marks in the rock, the scars left by the warriors' spears; two black-stained watercourses are the transformed bodies of two Liru. The fight centred on Mutitjulu (Maggie's Spring). Here a Kuniya woman fought using her *wana*; her features are preserved in the eastern face of the gorge. The features of the Liru warrior she attacked can be seen in the western face, where his eye, head wounds (transformed into vertical cracks), and severed nose form part of the cliff.

Lunpa, transformed into a boulder, eternally stares up at Kurrpanngu's paw prints on the face of Uluru.

Left: Pock marks on the south-west face of Uluru are scars left by the Liru warriors' spears; the two dark vertical streaks represent the transformed bodies of two Liru.

Right: The features of the Liru warrior that the Kuniya woman fought are preserved on the western face at Mutitjulu—note the severed nose.

Above Mutitjulu is Uluru rock hole. This is the home of a Kuniya who releases the water into Mutitjulu. If the flow stops during drought, the snake can be dislodged by standing at Mutitjulu and calling 'Kuka! Kuka! Kuka!' (Meat! Meat! Meat!). The journey to Uluru and the Liru snakes' attack are described in the public song cycle recording the Kuniya story.

Mita and Lunkata story
(The Blue-Tongue Lizards)

At Wangka Arrkal, on the border of South Australia beyond Mulga Park, two Bell-Bird brothers were stalking an emu. Disturbed, the animal ran northwards toward Uluru, where it was killed by Mita and Lungkata, Blue-Tongue Lizard men. The two Lizards cut up the emu meat with a stone axe at Kurumpa. Large joints of meat survive as a fractured slab of sandstone on the west side of Mutitjulu, but the Lizards buried the thigh at Kalaya Tjunta, (Emu Thigh) a spur on the south-east face of the Rock. When the Bell-Bird brothers arrived, the lizards handed them a skinny portion of their quarry, claiming that there was nothing else. In revenge, the hunters set fire to the Lizards' shelter. The two men attempted to escape by climbing the rock face, but they fell back and were burned to death. Lichen on the rock face at Mita Kampantja is the smoke from the fire, and the lizard men survive as two half-buried boulders.

Fractured slabs of sandstone on the west side of Mutitjulu represent joints of butchered emu meat.

The body of Lungkata. Smoke from the fire that killed him is visible behind.

(Harney 1968, para.2, p.9 and Mountford 1977, pp.38 and 138 both refer in error to Mita and Lungkata as a single figure, 'the sleepy lizard'.)

The Tjati story (The Red Lizard)

Tjati is a small, red lizard who lives on the mulga flats. In the creation period, he travelled to Uluru past Atila. When Tjati threw his *kali*, a curved throwing stick, it embedded itself in the north face of Uluru. Tjati scooped with his hands into the rock face to retrieve the *kali*, leaving a series of bowl-shaped hollows at Walaritja. Unable to recover his weapon, Tjati finally died in a cave at Kantju, where his other implements and bodily remains survive as large boulders on the cave floor. *Tjati* is the Yankuntjatjara name for the lizard the Pitjantjatjara call *lingka*.

The people

Uluru stands in the territory of Aboriginal people who speak a dialect called Yankuntjatjara. It is misleading to call the Yankuntjatjara a 'tribe', because like other such Aboriginal communities, they are not a politically unified group. Western European societies are based on centralised government; Aboriginal society is not. It is a society made up of small groups, each united by common descent from an ancestor and associated with an area of land that anthropologists refer to

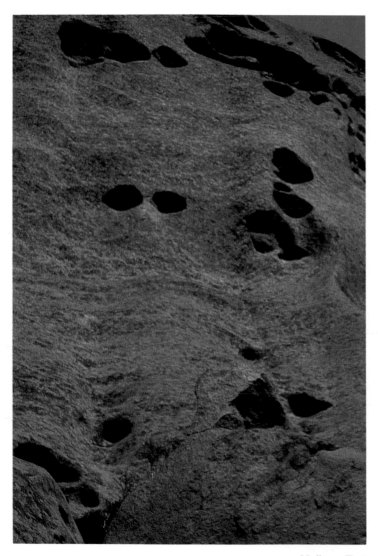

Cave where Tjati
died at Kantju.

Hollows Tjati
made at Walartja
when searching
for his throwing
stick.

as its estate (discussed further in Chapter 3). The
society is egalitarian in the strict sense of having
no overall leadership. Instead, each descent group
is linked to those around it, as equals, by many
cross-cutting economic, political and religious
obligations. These obligations are based on the
tjukurr, the Aboriginal law of the creation period.

Uluru is a point where the tracks of several ancestral groups cross each other. Atila (Mount Conner) and Katatjuta (the Olgas) are other crossroads on a network of dreaming tracks (the routes taken by ancestral heroes are generally referred to in Aboriginal English as 'dreaming tracks') that eventually tie together living desert peoples throughout central Australia. Each of these three points is like an island of water in a sea of sand: each was the refuge and base camp of a descent group made up of to two or three families, and the focus of these groups' estates. Under traditional Aboriginal law each group is obliged to look after the dreaming places, or sacred sites, created by the ancestral heroes in its estate, and to hand on the traditional songs, stories and ceremonies that commemorate the ancestors' adventures in that territory. Neighbouring groups help each other. Those whose estates lie on the same dreaming track share an obligation to protect and commemorate that tradition. Groups living over a wide area and owning many dreamings come together in ceremonies. In both ways, speakers of several dialects are united (Berndt 1959).

The most reliable map of Aboriginal dialects in the region is published in T.G.H. Strehlow's *Songs of Central Australia (1971)*. Alice Springs lies in the country of the Aranda, many of whom lived in the MacDonnell and surrounding ranges, enjoying an environment that is rich by central Australian

standards: a profusion of food plants and animals could be found along the semi-permanent waters trapped in river beds where they cut through the ranges. Aranda culture was greatly affected by its natural setting (Strehlow 1965 and 1969a). Along the south-west boundary of the Aranda speakers are found people known as Luritja. 'Luritja' is an Aranda term, said to mean 'strangers', used by speakers of the Kukatja and Mantuntatjara dialects to describe themselves. It is a name sometimes also adopted by the Pintupi of the desert further west. The traditional boundary between Aranda and Luritja was the Palmer River. The environment becomes increasingly harsh as one leaves the hills and enters open country beyond the Palmer. The Luritja separated the Aranda from speakers of dialects of the 'Western Desert' language used throughout large areas of Western and South Australia. Yankuntjatjara is one of these dialects. The best-studied of the dialects is that of their western neighbours, the Pitjantjatjara, whose name has been used in recent times as a label to describe all Western-Desert-language speakers living around the area where the borders of the Northern Territory, South and Western Australia meet. R.M. Berndt (1959) has described how Aborigines of the Western Desert often distinguish smaller communities within larger ones on the basis of progressively finer distinctions in dialect. When the anthropologists W. Baldwin Spencer and F.J. Gillen met Paddy Uluru's father at Uluru late in the nineteenth century, the Aboriginal man described himself as a Luritja, speaking presumably for the benefit of strangers whom he assumed to be unfamiliar with fine distinctions of local dialect (Spencer and Gillen 1912, p.114). In the 1930s, on the other hand, a police constable investigating the death of a young man from the Olgas at Mount Conner, recorded that Paddy Uluru and other men from the area called themselves Mulatjara. Mulatjara seems to be the name of a smaller community within Yankuntjatjara speakers. Neville Jones told me that, while working as Community Advisor at Docker River, he learnt of Mulatjara as a name for people whose country lay near Lake Amadeus. Pitjantjatjara speakers whose country is in the Petermann Ranges often similarly distinguish themselves from those in the Mann Ranges as the Pitja-pitja, a term also recorded by Jeremy Long (1963, p.7).

Traditions of the creation period

The ancestors who appear in the *inma* and 'myths' are described as men or women (*wati, minyma*); they used tools and weapons, but they also behaved in ways illuminated by their animal counterparts, as when the Possum ancestor of Katatjuta stole two Carpet Snake girls from Uluru and 'tied them up' with a love song in the way he clings to branches with his curling tail. Because

'myths' sometimes summarise the detail of the epic song cycles, different men may tell the same story in different ways, and on successive occasions one can learn more and more of the details in a narrative that at first seemed a simple 'just-so' story with little significance.

The stories of Uluru have already been recorded by C.P. Mountford, W.E. Harney and T.G.H. Strehlow. A careful comparison of what Bill Harney and Charles Mountford wrote shows that while Mountford recorded more details, the essentials are present in both accounts (*see* Appendix A). Harney (1968, 1969) makes a few mistakes, of which the most significant is his claim of a 'Mother Goddess' cult on the north face of the Rock, which seems to be derived from confusion over a Yam dreaming site, associated with a female ancestor, and some parts of the Hare Wallaby story. Strehlow (1969) was the only one of the three who appreciated the significance of the *inma*—an understanding gained from his deep knowledge of Aranda culture—but he withheld some of what he was told at Uluru out of respect for Aboriginal law.

Harney learnt about Uluru mainly from two men whose countries are in the Petermann Ranges, west of Uluru: Imalangu, or Harry Bigfoot, of Puta-Puta, and Snowy Minyintirri from beyond Docker River. Although Mountford's major informant was Palingka (or 'Lively'), an Uluru man, he first visited Uluru with men from the Mann Ranges (*see*

Mountford 1950). I worked principally with Paddy Uluru and Nipper Winmati. Both are Uluru men, and Nipper is Palingka's younger brother. Pompy Douglas, a man from the Musgrave Ranges who traced a link to Uluru through his mother's father was also particularly helpful in explaining these narratives and songs.

The significance of the legends

The view of the world expressed in the narratives gives meaning to many aspects of traditional social life. It is not dry history, but rather a vision of the order behind the world today.

The creation period, the *tjukurrpa*, is remembered as an age when the consequences of the heroes' behaviour established the form of the everyday world. The Mala community at Uluru is faced with a problem when it is invited, in the midst of its own celebrations, to attend those of another group. Its members' refusal to help the Wintalka men prepare for their dances is said to explain why today men from Uluru and Kikingkura wear different kinds of body decoration. Because the Mala fled from Uluru to Ulkiya, men from the two places are today related as brothers. Uluru and Kikingkura, however, stand in a relationship of brother-in-law to each other, and in recent generations there have been several marriages between the two groups.

The anti-social behaviour of the two Blue-Tongue Lizard men, Mita and Lungkata, illustrates what people think of those who refuse to divide meat with those entitled to share it, although the consequences were more dramatic than they might be in everyday life.

Atila lies on the boundary of the Yankuntjatjara and Matuntatjara speaking people. The two boys who quarrelled over the water which one, through his selfishness, concealed, originated this division. It was the selfish boy who, at Anari, first spoke Matuntatjara.

The ancestors' creative power could be directed through their artefacts, such as the boy's *tjuni*, which broke the ground to release water, or Tjati's *kali*, which buried itself in Uluru. Many of the artefacts that figure in these narratives are illustrated by Peter Brokensha in his study of Pitjantjatjara arts and crafts (Brokensha 1975); traditional stone tools, such as the *tjularrka* axe, are described by Bryan Hayden (1979).

The imagery of the songs gains much of its power from the parallels it draws between human behaviour and that of different animal species. *Tjinta-tjinta* the Willy Wagtail, for instance, is a bird with the disconcerting habit of puffing out its chest and swinging from side to side in a way that recalls the style of some men's dances. Among the songs of the Mala *inma* are verses describing the Tjinta-tjinta woman 'dancing like a man'. Another analogy is that of the Liru as raiding warriors. Liru is the name for poisonous snakes, a good metaphor for the party that attacked the peaceful Kuniya at Mutitjulu. As one learns deeper aspects of the *inma*, many of these parallels are developed into a profound concept of order in the world, which is revealed to young people through initiation.

The characters of the *tjukurrpa* form a community of individuals with different personalities and temperaments. Each Yankuntjatjara person is today identified from soon after birth with a specific ancestral being. The identity is based partly on the 'birth-place' (traditionally the place where the stub of the umbilical cord falls from the baby's belly), on or near a place associated with a particular ancestor; but older members of the living community look at the young child's physical features and character for further evidence of his personal dreaming. Paddy Uluru's father was identified with Lungkata, the Blue-Tongue. Pompy Douglas and his friend Pompy Wanampi, who were born on the same night at Anari and Wiputa, were identified with the Two Boys of the Dreamtime. Pompy Douglas remembers his older relatives telling him he would always quarrel with Wanampi, who in fact proved to be a good friend. One of the senior Kikingkura men, showing me a place where his dreaming had speared another member of the *tjukurrpa* community, commented with some pride, 'I'm a proper cranky bugger'. Tjalkalyiri, who claimed to have been born outside the Pulari cave on the

Rock's south face, identified himself as the son of Pulari.

Long family trees are not found in Yankuntjatjara or Pitjantjatjara society. By giving each individual a personal dreaming, the community constantly recreates the ancestral world. Past re-embodiments of a single ancestor fade into the collective image of that being; it is a tenet of the religion that on death a person becomes his dreaming. To die and be buried in one's own country ensures this will occur. During a visit to one of the most sacred sites at Uluru, one of the younger Kikingkura men spoke about the Rock's significance to Aboriginal people and said, pointing to the cliff face, 'That's a rock, but that's got to have something else, because that's got all those old men's memories inside'. Caves, standing stones and other sites associated with particular dreamings map the living community onto their land.

The idea that ancestral beings shaped the landscape is known to many White Australians through the concept of sacred sites. It is possible to think of the features at such sites as a photographic record of the ancestral saga, because a particular being leaves a visible imprint of his activities at a series of localities. Aboriginal people can point to them, saying, here is the mark of the Carpet Snake coming over the sandhills; here is the head pad on which she carried her eggs; here is the spear wound in her body. Each one of these places embodies a physical proof that the events of the *tjukurrpa* really did take place, but there is a crucial difference to a photograph; many of the sites preserving the mark of an ancestor also contain his or her spiritual power, a force that can be released through ritual. Particularly important are places where an ancestor went into the ground, often called Piti, such as Kuniya Piti and Mala Piti. Unless the ancestor in question is a malevolent being, like Kurrpanngu, places that hold its spiritual force should be kept clean of grass and other plants. Rubbing the rock will release some of the power and people closely associated with the place have a special responsibility for looking after it. It would be wrong to think that the ancestral narratives exist just to explain why particular caves or rocks have the shape they do; on the contrary, it is the caves and rocks that provide a means of expressing the ideas of Aboriginal religion.

On one occasion, Paddy Uluru and Nipper Winmati took two 12-year-old boys to one of the important Kuniya sites at Uluru. Paddy Uluru pulled up grass growing around the boulders that are the transformed remains of the Kuniya ancestors. Both men talked approvingly of how, when he was Ranger, Bill Harney had helped to keep the site clean. Winmati told the two boys to sit astride one boulder and rest their hands on it. Uluru swept the boulders with a bunch of grass.

With their hands both men then rubbed the boulder on which the boys were sitting. Winmati explained: 'When we're hungry, we rub the stone to make big *kuniya*'. I saw similar actions at other sites around the Rock (*compare* Gould 1968, p.115).

The existence of sites throughout the desert associated with the network of dreaming tracks also organises the landscape in a very practical way. David Lewis (1976) discovered how desert people navigated during bush journeys through their knowledge of where their destination lay, and where they themselves stood, in relation to conspicuous story places. Travelling with Paddy Uluru and others, we periodically climbed sandhills to check our location against landmarks invisible from the gullies. Contrary to Lewis's experience, I found people could even navigate in the dark, with only the outline of hills against the stars to guide them. On one occasion, we located an isolated soak on the Mala track, which no one had visited for many years, because people knew which course the Mala ancestors had taken between more familiar sites recorded in the Mala Inma, and they knew the site must lie on that line.

The *tjukurrpa* is the foundation for Aboriginal peoples' lives; it is a law that underlies everything they do and see around them. As they sometimes say, contrasting their own law with ours, 'White Man's law is just paper'.

CHAPTER 2

Living off the land

Aboriginal people have probably lived around Uluru for over 10 000 years. Excavations in the James Range, 80 kilometres east of Alice Springs, produced material more than 10 000 years old (Gould n.d., p.8), and the more recent excavation at Puntutjarpa, 400 kilometres west of Uluru, in Western Australia, uncovered camp debris shown by radiocarbon dating to be about 10 200 years old (Gould 1971, p.165). Richard Gould found that, despite small changes in the stone tools of different ages in Puntutjarpa rockshelter, the evidence was generally of 'a stable hunting and foraging way of life which can be regarded as the Australian desert culture' (Gould 1971, p.174).

The culture was a subsistence one; that is, the people produced all they needed locally and, unlike the Europeans who brought the pastoral economy to central Australia, did not specialise in the production of single foods. The only things traded were ceremonial items, such as pearl shell from Australia's north coast. To supply all their needs from the semi-desert in which they live, people must know where to look for many different animals and plants, and where water, scarce as it is, can be found.

Pitjantjatjara dialects recognise at least four distinct types of country: the mulga flats, open sand dunes, rocky hills and the encircling trees around rock faces such as those at Uluru. Each must be visited from time to time to obtain vital resources—different parts of the bush favour

17

different plant species and animals also have their favoured habitats. Water is never present in large quantities. Rain falls irregularly to fill rock holes among the hills and replenish soaks in dry creek beds, where the sand can be dug away until water seeps into the hole. The Aborigines moved opportunistically, retiring to base camps in drought, spreading out after rain.

Useful plants

The semi-desert country around Uluru is a varied one. In open country, sandhills alternate with low-lying flats, and many useful plants grow in each environment. Spinifex, desert oaks and light scrub grow on the windblown sand of the dunes, and mulga grows on the intervening flats. According to Peter Latz (1978, p.81), the largest variety of food plants is found on the sandhills, yet this is also the habitat where drinking water is most scarce.

Mulga seeds were ground for flour. Mulga wood is used to make spear-throwers, throwing sticks and coolamons (wooden bowls). The Ayers Rock mulga grows long, straight branches, which are shaped into heavy stabbing spears called *winta*. The roots of the witchetty bush, which also grows on mulga flats, are dug up and broken open to take out the witchetty grubs: one side of the bush growing less well than the other is a sign that grubs are in the roots. Another clue is the

Above: Desert oak country.
Below: Mulga country.

Left: Digging up witchetty grubs from the roots of an *ilkuwara* bush, using an iron *wana*.

Right: Close-up of witchetty grub.

presence of discarded skins of adult insects that have emerged. The seeds of woolly-butt grass and 'native millet', which also grow in mulga country, were harvested and ground to make flour, from which unleavened bread was baked in the ashes of a fire. The red flowers of the *Eremophila* bush are filled with a sugary nectar, which can be sucked from the base of the flower.

In the sandhills, different types of plant can be found growing on the ridges and in the hollows. On the ridges grow a grevillea with nectar-filled flowers, and also wild 'plum' trees. The *Gyrostemon* tree provides lightweight timber for carving carrying dishes. Emu-poison bush provided poison which was put in water where emus came to drink; the leaves of *ilpara*, waterbush, were burnt to an ash and mixed with the 'chewing tobacco' picked from the base of rock faces at Uluru. In the hollows, at the foot of desert oaks, grows a solanum with an edible fruit, sometimes called a wild tomato, which is considered to taste like a grape. Spinifex grass provides natural gum, which was used to mount the stone blade on the end of a spear-thrower. The desert 'poplar', a botanical relative of *Gyrostemon*, also grows in the sandhills, and its soft wood is sometimes used for animal carvings.

The steep rock faces of Uluru and Katatjuta harbour different species: *Ilyi*, the rock fig and a wild 'plum', which, although classed botanically with the sandhill species, is given a different name by the Pitjantjatjara. The tumbled boulders at the foot of rock faces are the source of 'chewing tobacco', and light hunting spears are made from the spear bush, *urtjanpa*.

In the Petermanns and Musgraves, more gentle hill slopes predominate. Here distinctive species of acacia grow, including *utjalpara*, a source of witchetty grubs and a sweet gum exuded by insects which Aboriginal children liked to suck. One middle-aged man explained, 'I often got a lolly from that one when I was a little boy'.

Rain falling on the vast expanses of bare rock at Uluru, Katatjuta and smaller outcrops flows out across the surrounding soil before soaking away. These sheet-flooding zones harbour flourishing colonies of bloodwood trees. Bloodwood provides

Mingkulpa (wild tobacco) growing at Uluru.

Left: *Ilyi* (rock figs) near Mutitjulu.

Right: *Wakati* (*Portulaca oleracea*) growing in mulga zone.

timber for making several types of coolamon, including the deep bowls called *piti*, the scoops called *wirra*, and spear-throwers. Between the bloodwoods can be found a low, crawling plant with a red, fleshy stem called *wakati*, which bears a seed that was ground to make flour. The grass *kunakanti* , which also has edible seeds, grows here, as does an edible solanum. Different species of eucalypt grow beside creeks: *Apara*, river red gum (*Eucalyptus camaldulensis*), grows along Britten-Jones Creek and gives its name to the soak, creek and country, Aparanya; in the vicinity of Docker River, the ghost gum (*Eucalyptus papuana*) also occurs. River red gum and ghost gum provide wood for coolamons and other artefacts.

Animal habitats

Many animals tend to live in only one of these plant habitats. The red kangaroo is restricted to level grassland and is mainly found on the mulga flats; the euro feeds in spinifex on hill and rock slopes (Frith 1973, pp.273 and 281). Although the emu lives in sandhill country, it was often caught near water, either by covering the main rock hole with stones and poisoning smaller pools, or by spearing the birds as they came to drink. Men hid behind artificial stone hides or natural boulders, because emus which drank poisoned water would try to regurgitate and the hunters had to rush out to wrestle with the birds, keeping their beaks shut.

Change in subsistence activities

Some plants, such as spinifex and the wild plum, grow in more than one habitat, and resources such as nectar or wood for coolamons and spear-throwers can be obtained from more than one species, but each habitat must have been regularly exploited for its unique resources. The disappearance of traditional subsistence activities would have as big an impact on the region's ecology as the extinction of one of the main animal species, but Aboriginal people still rely on the bush for many things. Kangaroo and euro meat are preferred to beef; so is rabbit. Artefacts for sale are still made from traditional materials.

Witchetty grubs are enjoyed. At Kikingkura outstation we saw edible berries harvested. Although this was not done regularly by the people living at Uluru, children were quick to pick wild 'plums' and 'tomatoes' when they could, during expeditions to the sandhills.

One of the biggest changes since White contact has been the disappearance of controlled burning of the bush. Peter Latz (1978) writes that many of the most important food plants appear during the early stages of regrowth after minor fires, and that controlled burning of small patches of bush was an everyday part of foraging expeditions. Early explorers repeatedly found parties of Aboriginal people firing the land. Since people have been gathered into missions or settled around station homesteads, regular burning has largely ceased. In the 1970s, several years of good rainfall caused a build up of inflammable scrub, grass and branches, resulting in disastrous wildfires that swept over wide areas in the Uluru National Park during 1976.

Aboriginal diet has also changed since contact. It is thought that when people were entirely dependent on the bush for food, meat made up only 20 to 30 per cent of the diet (see Gould 1969a). With traditional weapons, animals such as kangaroo or euro were hard to catch. Paddy Uluru once recalled how as a young man he had killed a kangaroo at Tjulu (now the site of Curtin Springs homestead) and carried it back to Uluru, a distance of 80 kilometres. Richard Gould, living with people in the bush in Western Australia during 1966 to 1967, found that the women produced an average of 4.5 kilograms of vegetable food each day, devoting 4½ hours to collection and 2½ hours to preparation, while the men found only lizards. Although reliable, collecting vegetable foods could be hard work. Peter Brokensha asked Pitjantjatjara women living at an outstation from Amata to make damper from wild millet, *kaltu kaltu* (Brokensha 1975, p.25). He found that to gather less than 2 kilograms of seed from an area within 1 kilometre of their camp took three women 3 hours. To grind, winnow and cook the seed took another 2 hours. Although, as he says, there was a mad scramble among the camp's children for a piece of the cooking, it is not surprising that purchased flour has almost completely replaced indigenous sources. At Yuendumu in the mid-1970s, almost 30 per cent by weight of purchased food was flour; at Yalata a family of five would buy 11 kilograms of white flour a week (figures cited in Peterson 1978, p.32; *see also* Rose 1965, pp.31-2; Cutter 1978, p.67 and Brokensha 1975, p.25).

The amount of meat obtained from the bush has, on the other hand, probably increased, not only because guns are more effective than spears, but also because cattle grazing and bore water help kangaroos to flourish (Frith 1978, p.90). The introduced rabbit has also become a major source of meat. At Brokensha's outstation, rabbits were eaten practically all the time (1975). W.V. MacFarlane, who briefly visited two outstations in Western Australia during the 1960s, records that at Kutjuntari seven euros were shot in eight days, and at Warawiya the men, using .22 rifles 'brought in a kangaroo almost *every day*' (1978, pp.51 and 54).

Appendix C lists the observed hunting trips made by people at Uluru during the period of my fieldwork. There is no reason to think the euro or the kangaroo, let alone the rabbit, is threatened, because people's subsistence needs limit the amount of hunting. The only threat to natural resources seems to be that of commercial exploitation. D. Roff suggests that the brushtail possum became locally extinct during early contact times because too many were killed to sell their skins to White men (1976, p.15). Sedentary life also exacerbates the local depletion of resources around camps, which is one of the reasons people in settlements rely more on purchased foods. N.B. Tindale's comments on traditional camps (quoted below) suggest that this may always have been a problem.

Traditional artefacts

Traditional Western Desert tools and implements have been described by Brokensha (1975) and B. Hayden (1979). Brokensha describes how the spear-thrower is made from a slab of wood split

Mulga tree at Witapula bears old scar from slab removal.

from a mulga tree using metal tools; Hayden described how stone tools were used for the same purpose. The same technique is used to obtain wood for wooden bowls, throwing sticks and other implements. Paddy Uluru used axe blades as far as possible as wedges rather than cutting tools, paralleling the way in which Hayden shows stone wedges and axes to have been used. This technique does not kill the tree from which the wood is obtained. Both Hayden and Brokensha describe how digging sticks and spears are made. Only the straightest of *urtjanpa* limbs are suitable for making spears. They are cut at the base and pulled downwards out of the tangled mass of intertwined branches. Twigs must be trimmed off, traditionally with a stone adze, like those mounted on spear-throwers, and the stem straightened by warming it in a fire.

Distribution of water

The availability of water determined which parts of the bush could be exploited at any time. After rain, people moved from secure water supplies around base camps to isolated or temporary waters in the surrounding country, where numerous resources could then be gathered. George Silberbauer (1971) suggests that 231 points (58 mm) of rain are needed in a summer month, and 58 points (14.5 mm) in a winter month, to produce plant foods. Table 1 documents local rainfall over a fifteen-year period.

Yankuntjatjara and Pitjantjatjara recognise four principal sources of available water. The most reliable are the *wanampitjara* or springs, but the quality of spring water is not good, since it has soaked into the ground at the foot of the ranges and picked up many salts while flowing underground towards the centre of artesian basins. The term *wanampitjara* might be translated as 'having a Rainbow Serpent', although aboriginal people generally refer to *wanampi* simply as 'water snakes'. The wanampi are a class of legendary beings who carry water underground from one available source to another. One wanampi made Britten-Jones Creek as he crawled north from the Musgrave Ranges, diving below the sandhills, where the creek fades out, and re-emerging at Katiti (Bobby's Well), on the shore of Lake Amadeus. Old men said that when Katiti is cleaned out, seeds of the callitris tree, which only grows in the Musgrave Ranges can be found. Springs may have a double significance in legend: the presence of a wanampi is indicated by the underground source, and the well that taps this supply is the imprint of an ancestral being, as when Anari was created by the boy's club. Natural springs were important in helping pastoral settlement of the area, but their Matuntatjara and Yankuntjatjara names have frequently been recorded on the topographic maps, such as Calatta (Kulata) Springs, Murrathurra (Marutjara)

Looking into
Purrarra well.

Table 1 **Rainfall recorded at Curtin Springs homestead 1960–77** (in millimetres)

	Month	1960	1961	1962	1963	1964	1965	1966	1967	1968	1969	1970	1971	1972	1973	1974	1975	1976	1977	Monthly average
SUMMER	January	23.6	6.3	50.0	—	9.3	—	3.6	27.9	56.6	26.1	—	5.3	2.8	**60.4**	**258.9**	13.2	24.6	—	31.6
	February	6.2	—	—	—	—	—	5.1	**84.8**	8.1	**153.8**	—	—	—	21.6	**134.5**	21.8	36.0	**93.0**	31.4
	March	—	—	4.3	2.8	—	5.3	0.3	**141.1**	21.6	53.3	2.8	34.0	**81.2**	3.8	3.3	4.1	—	54.0	22.9
WINTER	April	**27.7**	**37.5**	—	3.5	**38.8**	—	12.2	—	**40.6**	1.3	10.4	—	—	3.8	**145.4**	1.5	—	—	17.9
	May	**21.0**	—	10.3	**27.8**	7.3	1.0	9.4	11.4	**69.0**	4.8	**16.8**	—	—	10.9	**33.0**	—	—	8.6	12.9
	June	—	—	4.0	**19.5**	1.3	1.5	**48.2**	—	**96.2**	14.7	—	10.9	—	**42.6**	—	—	—	—	13.3
	July	3.8	—	7.0	3.0	—	1.5	—	—	**45.4**	3.0	—	—	1.0	**74.1**	7.1	**14.7**	—	—	8.9
	August	—	3.5	10.8	—	—	**18.0**	10.7	—	**21.8**	—	—	**18.0**	**14.5**	**28.9**	**30.5**	**65.0**	—	3.3	12.5
	September	—	—	—	—	**20.8**	7.5	—	—	5.6	8.1	**19.3**	**14.5**	**15.7**	9.1	**43.9**	**66.2**	1.3	3.8	12.0
SUMMER	October	27.6	—	48.8	—	22.3	2.3	10.9	—	6.6	36.8	0.8	—	—	9.9	**108.6**	43.1	**57.9**	34.1	22.7
	November	—	1.3	—	—	7.8	12.8	27.4	14.0	20.8	4.1	29.7	**88.3**	9.4	3.6	38.3	**62.7**	0.6	48.0	20.5
	December	3.8	—	1.3	10.0	2.8	4.8	**67.0**	—	7.9	**67.3**	7.9	8.9	—	5.3	17.3	48.7	1.7	10.6	14.8
	Annual total	113.7	48.6	136.5	66.6	110.4	54.7	195.0	279.3	400.2	373.3	87.7	179.9	124.6	273.5	820.8	341.0	122.0	255.4	Annual average 221.3 (8.7 inches)

Note: Figures in bold type are those that would have allowed foraging expeditions in peripheral country. See comment on G.B. Silberbauer in text. Rainfall figures kindly made available by Peter Severin.

Well, Bogga-bogga (Paku-paku) Well, Anari and Purrarra.

A soak, *kakanpa*, is also fed from an underground supply, but in this case it is a superficial and purely local water table in the sand of a dry creek bed or soil on the margin of a rock dome. In the MacDonnell Ranges, large permanent pools collect in the shaded bends of rivers, but the Petermann and Musgrave Ranges lack these oases. The location of a soak can often be spotted from a short distance by the excavated hollow, half a metre or so in depth, that has been dug to reach the water. In cattle country, these hollows collapse into shallow depressions with the trampling of the animals' hoofs after rain. Soaks are fairly reliable, because the water lies beneath

Left: Soak at Waltjarr on the north side of Aputjilpi.

Right: Soak at Witapula trampled by animal hoofs after rain. Atila (Mount Conner) is seen on horizon.

Rock hole at Patji.

the ground surface, where it is protected from evaporation. When looking for a site for the mission eventually established at Ernabella, J.R.B. Love was struck by how few sources of water there were in the Petermann Reserve and how little many of them held. At Kunapanti, the Aboriginal men with him dug out a tiny soak, two feet deep and a foot across. After each man had had a small drink the dogs scrambled in. The women and children had to wait for the water level to rise before they too were able to drink (Love & Balfour 1937, pp.13–14).

A rock hole, *tjukula*, is not protected by sand or soil. Rock holes occur on exposed platforms in the gullies of Uluru and Katajuta and the ranges.

There are numerous rock holes in the Kelly Hills, the Petermanns and Musgraves. There is also one at Patji, midway between Uluru and the Musgraves.

The most transient of water sources is the claypan, *tjintjira*. Claypans have a large surface area in relation to their depth—the opposite of rock holes—so they are particularly vulnerable to evaporation. Because the water is held up by a deposit of clay, none percolates through to be conserved in the underlying sand. H.H. Finlayson wrote with feeling: 'bitter is the disappointment of those who attempt to dig soaks in the pans when the water is gone', but he added, 'while it lasts, however, the milky clay-impregnated water is deliciously sweet' (1935, p.25).

Water sources in sandhill country are often associated with substantial camp sites. These are typically located in a depression on one of the neighbouring dunes, the rim of the dune forming a natural windbreak. Such a camp may be up to 50 metres long, the surface littered with stone flakes and grindstones, among which can be identified *kanti*, small flakes of quartz or 'opal' of the type mounted for use as adze blades. *Tjularrka* are larger cutting tools, made from fine-grained rock, such as basalt, and used as knives to butcher meat (the Blue Tongue Lizard men used a *tjularrka* to cut up their stolen emu), or as a wedge in splitting wood for spear-throwers and so on. The *tjiwa* is a flat rock used as a lower

grindstone; the *tjungari* is a round one making the upper grindstone. When the soak or rock hole is surrounded by a rock platform, polished hollows can be seen on the rock margin where people have used it as a *tjiwa*, wetting and grinding grass or mulga-seed and allowing it to fall into a coolamon.

The camp site generally lies about 200 metres from water. Finlayson noticed that frequent camping near isolated soaks and rock holes altered the vegetation, destroying timber and increasing the growth of what he termed 'small herbage' (1935, p.105). N.B. Tindale (1972, pp.242–4) interprets such local over-exploitation as a reason for moving the camp site away, but Richard Gould (1968, p.105) suggests two other reasons for separating camp from water: to prevent camp noises frightening game animals who come to drink, and to let relatives who should avoid each other all use the water.

Left: Rock surface used as lower grindstone.
Right: *Tjungari* and *tjiwa* at Patji.

Pompy Douglas
demonstrates
grinding
technique.

Foraging patterns

Recollections of older people suggest that, in the 'green time' after rain, the whole group living at a base camp might move out to one of the peripheral camps near a soak or rock hole. People describe traditional life as one of alternately travelling (*ananyi*) and sitting or camping (*nyinanyi*), a pattern summarised in the characteristic central Australian art motif of circles linked by parallel lines (*see* Munn 1973). Midway between base camps lie waters shared by those who would approach from either side. Paddy Uluru remembers meeting Tjalkalyiri at Patji when they were children. He had walked from Uluru with his parents; Tjalkalyiri arrived, riding on his father's shoulders, from Apara in the northern Musgraves.

In good seasons, major ceremonial gatherings took place at base camps, attended by up to two hundred people. The reports of explorers and travellers before 1930 give insights into this pattern of behaviour, and it is possible, using the place names recorded in these reports, to identify which encounters took place at base camps and which groups were met foraging across the intervening country (*see* Table 3). Groups consisting of one or two families are met at both base camps and in marginal country, while groups of over a hundred are (with one exception recorded by W.E.P. Giles) seen only at base camps.

Regular walking routes traversed the bush. People based at Uluru were linked to those at Atila, Aputjilpi (the Kelly Hills), Apara and Kulpitjata (in the northern Musgrave Ranges), Muntarurra (in the Olia Chain) and Katatjuta by a circular series of paths, which members of all these groups followed in good seasons (Figure 1 shows the routes taken). Paddy Uluru and other older men were able to give the times it took to travel along these walking routes (Table 2), but of course people often foraged as they went, especially in zones around the marginal waters, where they might pause for a week or more. Toby Nangina, for instance, talked of walking from Uluru to Atila 'not going straight but by Katiti and Tjilpil, carrying a big coolamon on the head'. Richard Gould (1969b) has described the foraging expeditions that he accompanied.

When Baldwin Spencer and F.J. Gillen visited Uluru in 1894, they met a man whose name they recorded as 'Lungkatitukukana' (1912, pp.114–5). This is almost certainly Paddy Uluru's father, Lungkata Tjukurrpa (the name means Blue-Tongue Lizard Dreaming). He was with his two wives and three children, probably before Paddy Uluru was born. Spencer and Gillen travelled with this family to Katatjuta. During the outward journey they were astonished to see how quickly the older wife could dig for honey ants; she soon dug a hole big enough to hold her body. Unfortunately for her, the honey ants were kept as

Sand hill campsite at Patji.

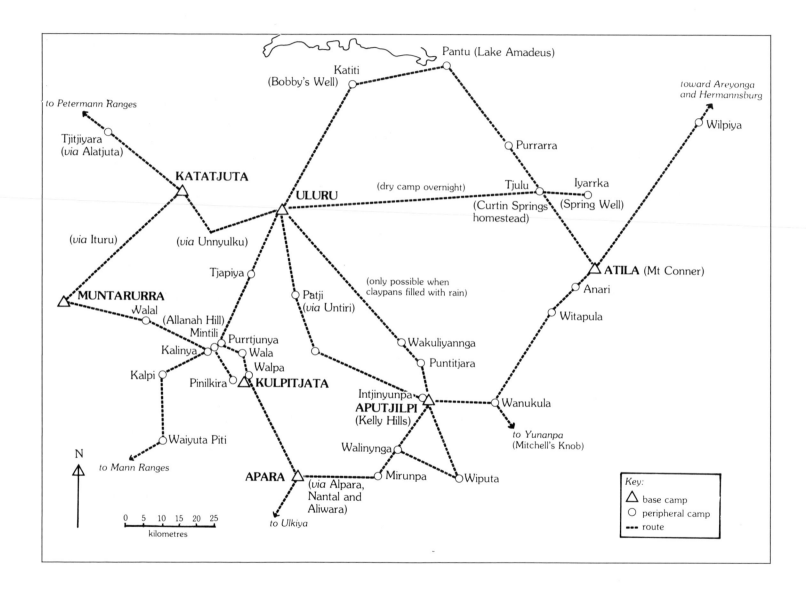

Figure 1

Traditional
walking routes
between Uluru
and adjacent
estates

to Petermann Ranges

Tjitjiyara
(*via* Alatjuta)

KATATJUTA

(*via* Ituru)

(*via* Unnyulku)

MUNTARURRA

Walal

(Allanah Hill)

Mintili

Purrtjunya

Kalinya

Wala

Walpa

Kalpi

Pinilkira

KULPITJATA

Waiyuta Piti

to Mann Ranges

APARA

(*via* Alpara,
Nantal and
Aliwara)

to Ulkiya

Tjapiya

Patji
(*via* Untiri)

Wakuliyannga

Puntitjara

Intjinyunpa

APUTJILPI
(Kelly Hills)

Walinynga

Mirunpa

Wiputa

to Yunanpa
(Mitchell's Knob)

Wanukula

Katiti
(Bobby's Well)

Pantu (Lake Amadeus)

Purrarra

ULURU

(dry camp overnight)

Tjulu

Iyarrka

(Curtin Springs
homestead)

(Spring Well)

(only possible when
claypans filled with rain)

ATILA (Mt Conner)

Anari

Witapula

*toward Areyonga
and Hermannsburg*

Wilpiya

N

0 5 10 15 20 25
kilometres

Key:
△ base camp
○ peripheral camp
---- route

specimens by the two White men. 'It must have been rather a severe trial', they wrote, 'to watch the honey ants, which they dug out, being transferred to the collecting bottle' (1912, p.123). At Katatjuta, Spencer and Gillen were introduced by Lungkatitukukana to a group of several families camped in bough shades (huts built from branches). On the return journey,

Lungkatitukukana's family was observed burning spinifex and catching small animals such as lizards that were driven out. They were also lucky enough to catch two kangaroos.

The typical foraging range of families associated with a particular base camp extended at least to adjacent base camps, so that neighbouring groups overlapped in their use of the bush. Figure 4

Table 2   **Time required to cover traditional walking routes**

Journey	Time	Route	Distance
Patji to Uluru	Leave Patji before sunrise	Direct	23 km
Uluru to Tjulu	Overnight	Leave Uluru in the early evening, make a 'dry' camp away from water during the night and arrive at Tjulu the following morning	73 km
Kulpitjata to Uluru	Half a day	Leaving from a camp 'just north of Kulpitjata' (this time seems exceptionally fast)	48 km
Uluru to Apara	One day	Via water at Walpi, Walal and Alpara; first and last are on Apara Creek	80 km
Apara to Ulkiya*	One day	Via Apatiri soak and Kanyala Mitu rock hole	45 km
Uluru to Mintili	One day +	Via Tjapiya; camp overnight at Tjapiya; Tjapiya to Mintili takes one day, even though looking for sugar ant and goanna	Uluru–Tjapiya 20 km Tjapiya–Mintili 23 km
Uluru to Katatjuta	One day	Via Unnyulku	37 km (approx.)
Katatjuta to Tjitjiyara	One day	Via Alatjuta rock hole	
Aputjilpi to Uluru	One day and one night	Via Kaltiti and Patji rock holes	75 km

*Note. Not possible to walk from Uluru to Ulkiya in hot season.

shows the extent of typical foraging trips from Uluru, according to Paddy Uluru and from Kikingkura, as described by Leslie Mintjantji; both men's lives were unaffected by White intrusion until they were young adults. They pointed out that longer journeys were sometimes made to attend ceremonies. Leslie Mintjantji had walked as far as Apara; Paddy Uluru, to Ulkiya (south of the Musgrave Ranges) and beyond. While staying at others' base camps, it was possible to meet groups who approached from the opposite direction; at Apara, for instance, people from Uluru met families from Ulkiya, and Piltati in the Mann Ranges.

Sometimes the water at a base camp was exhausted. In bad years the people belonging to Kulpitjata had to join those at Apara. Those at Katatjuta had to move to Uluru. Spencer and Gillen found much less water at Katatjuta than W.E.P. Giles's account of a running stream flowing away to the south had led them to expect; all that Lungkatitukukana could show them was a small pool less than a yard in diameter. Peter Severin of Curtin Springs reported that, during the drought of the late 1950s and early 1960s, Maggie's Spring (Mutitjulu) was dry. As Spencer and Gillen concluded, 'It is most unsafe to speak of any waterhole in Central Australia as permanent' (1912, p.126). The unpredictability of rain is exacerbated by an underlying cycle of general drought alternating with relatively rich years.

There have been major droughts in 1890–91, 1915–17, 1931–39, 1946–48 and 1958–66.

Table 1 showed how wet and dry periods follow each other unpredictably, as the Centre is subject to the chance fluctuations of weather patterns originating in the tropics of the north coast or more temperate regions to the far south. Richard Gould points out that conditions in one part of the Western Desert might allow more than a hundred to gather for a ceremony, while elsewhere drought forced people to remain scattered in family groups (1968, p.103). Other writers have described how sharp the dividing line can be between an area stricken by drought and one that has received good rain. Bill Harney recorded a journey he made through the Centre with an Aboriginal party in 1952. As they travelled, they were told of an area ahead where rain had recently fallen. After surviving a dust storm, they came to the promised country. Harney remembered, 'From the red to the green was but a matter of a bare mile. On one side despair, on the other a happiness that overwhelmed us as we moved through a wealth of wild flowers' (1969, p.148). Charles Duguid went with T.G.H. Strehlow to the Petermann Ranges in 1939 to investigate the effects of a long drought. He was struck by the abundance of kangaroo, wallaby and emu in the Musgrave Ranges, which had not been affected, and their absence in the Petermanns. Petermann Aborigines they met said they had been living solely on 'wild cucumber' and the roots of *yalka* grass, which they found on the banks of the dry creeks. Near Ernabella, Duguid and Strehlow met an emaciated group from the Petermanns, approaching safely after a long journey from the drought. The one Ernabella man leading them to the mission was easily distinguished by his healthy condition (Duguid 1972, p.136). On the basis of his work at Balgo, R.M. Berndt considers that people might be forced to move up to 300 kilometres from their home territory during drought (1972, p.183).

Although people no longer regularly use the

traditional walking routes or peripheral camps, their distribution and the customary patterns of use induced by the difficult conditions of the desert are important elements in contemporary Aboriginal land ownership. It is not a matter of large areas being uninhabitable, but one of an environment that provides a range of choices that allows people to forage and camp over a wide area of varying plant and animal habitats. This is reflected in the pattern of rights to land that has persisted to the present.

Table 3 **Size of Aboriginal groups encountered by early explorers and travellers**
(*see* Figure 1 for location of base camps mentioned)

Year	Base camps	Peripheral camps	Source
1873	Camp fires seen at Uluru; two young men come to get water	—	W.E.P. Giles 1889, entry for 3 August 1873
	Three people from the Aboriginal camp Visit W.C. Gosse's camp at Uluru	—	Entry for 4 August 1873
1874	—	Men hunting encountered between Puta-Puta and Piltati. 'A great number' chase Giles and his companion.	W.E.P. Giles 1889, vol. 2, pp.7–8
	—	'Half a dozen' people approach Giles's camp at eastern end of Petermanns	vol. 2, p.58
	Visited by a group of three men at Uluru		vol. 2, p.65
	Found 'The whole tribe of the Petermanns' close to Piltati	—	vol. 2, p.324

Year	Base camps	Peripheral camps	Source
1889	—	Explorers followed by four Aboriginal people near western end of *Pantu* (Lake Amadeus)	W.H. Tietkins 1891, p.51
	Several camp fires sighted at Katatjuta	—	p.55
1894	Met a man called 'Lungkartitukukana' (Paddy Uluru's father, Lungkata Tjukurrpa) with his two wives and three children at Uluru.	—	W.B. Spencer and F.J. Gillen 1912, p.114
	Met several families camped in bough shades at Katatjuta	—	p.125
1903	Six men, one woman and two children found camping at Apara	—	H. Basedow 1914
	—	Group of two men, two women and two children camped at soak north of Aputjilpi	p.172
	—	Party of three men, three women and five children camped at Puntitjara, on east side of Aputjilpi	p.173 and plate 47
1906	—	'Kamaran's Well' near Pantu, two old men and five young ones encountered.	F.R. George, diary entry for 21 February 1906
1926	Thirty-five people accompany Mackay's party from Katatjuta to Kulapurunya Hills	—	D. Mackay 1926, p.5
	—	Four people camped at Ituntu, in Puta-puta country	D. Mackay 1929, p.263
	—	A large camp found on Irving Creek, between Puta-puta and Piltati	p.263
	Several parties of Aboriginal people arrive at Piltati, including old men in charge of boys to be initiated	—	D. Mackay 1926, p.8

Year	Base camps	Peripheral camps	Source
1930	'400' people assembled for ceremony near Kikingkura	—	M. Terry, n.d., pp.57–9
1931	—	Two men, four women and several children found a few miles from Piltati, waiting in camp for others to return from foraging; thirty-three people in camp by nightfall	W. Gill 1968, p.88
	130 people at ceremony near Kikingkura	—	p.110
1933	A large group assembled near Kikingkura for ceremony	—	F. Clune 1942, p.278
1939	One man and his son met at Piltati (after severe drought)	—	C. Duguid 1972, p.133
	Three men, four women and three children met near Kikingkura	—	p.134
		Other small parties encountered in the Petermanns to a total of twenty-six people	p.135

CHAPTER 3

Land ownership

The Pitjantjatjara and Yankuntjatjara did not move at random across the country. Rights to specific areas of land are held by groups of people linked by common descent, although not always through lines transmitted from father to son. Each group holds rights to an area that can be called its estate (Stanner 1965, p.2). The estate is focused on the group's base camp and takes its name either from the reliable water source near that camp, or from the district within which the camp lies. Uluru takes its name from Uluru rock hole, above Mutitjulu (Maggie's Spring), and Apara takes its name from Apara soak, in the bed of a creek surrounded by river red gums. Other estates acquire their names from conspicious hills, such as Katatjuta (many heads) from the Olgas, and Aputjilpi (grey rocks) from the Kelly Hills. Each estate also possesses a number of less reliable or more brackish peripheral water sources.

In practice, the land between water sources is as important as the water itself and is often still regularly exploited for food and wood.

The most important right which the Aboriginal owners of an estate possessed was the right to punish women, children or strangers who trespassed on their sacred sites. The punishment was likely to be death. Although neighbouring groups have the right to forage over each others' estates, the owners hold certain privileges. Several times I witnessed men voluntarily handing over a portion of what they had gathered to another, who was owner of the estate in which they had been foraging. Once, when Paddy Uluru collected spear-bush from the Olgas, he gave half to Napala Jack. Napala explained, 'Katatjuta, that's my country'. Another time, Uluru picked *pitjuri* when we returned to the Rock and gave this to Napala instead. It seems likely that people used fire to signal their presence to other groups in the area (see Chapter 6).

Where peripheral sites were shared by two or more groups, then their estates overlap. The soak at Tjapiya, for instance, belongs to both Uluru and Kulpitjata, the most northerly estate in the Musgraves. Patji is shared by Uluru, Kulpitjata and Apara. The hill Yulpartji (SF 52-12 388754) is shared by Apara and Ulkiya. Figure 2 combines all the information obtained about the ownership of places that can be precisely located on the map; it shows that there is frequent overlap on the edges of estates.

People do not consider that estates have precise boundaries: they merge into those around them. In his original essay on Aboriginal estates W.E.H. Stanner (1965, pp.11-12) recognised this when he wrote that precise and rigid boundaries between mutually exclusive estates would be inconsistent with the known patterns of movement and intergroup relations in Aboriginal society. This is particularly so in the harsh conditions of the Western Desert. In effect, each site has a circular zone of bush accessible to exploitation from it,

and each site is linked to other sites by the corridors along which people moved. The point at which bush became inaccessible from a given base would depend on such things as weather conditions and the stamina of individuals. Other anthropologists who have studied territorial organisation in the desert areas of central Australia have earlier come to similar conclusions: an estate is a cluster of sites rather than a bounded block of land (Berndt 1959, pp.96-8; 1972, p.182; O'Connell 1976, p.5).

Ownership of Uluru

Both Bill Harney and C.P. Mountford believed that Aboriginal ownership of Uluru was divided between two groups. Harney seems to have reached this conclusion after he was told that the south side of the Rock belonged to the 'Shade Side' people, the north side to the 'Sun Side' people (Harney 1969, pp.76-7). Harney thought that a man inherited membership of one of these two categories from his mother (1969, p.77), but they are in fact generational divisions: that is, all the people in one generation belong to the 'Sun Side', all their children to the 'Shade Side', and their grandchildren to the 'Sun Side' again (cf. Gould 1969b, p.106; Munn 1965, p.7). In men's ritual, members of either category may sit and work together, but it is obvious that any of the descent groups owning an estate will contain

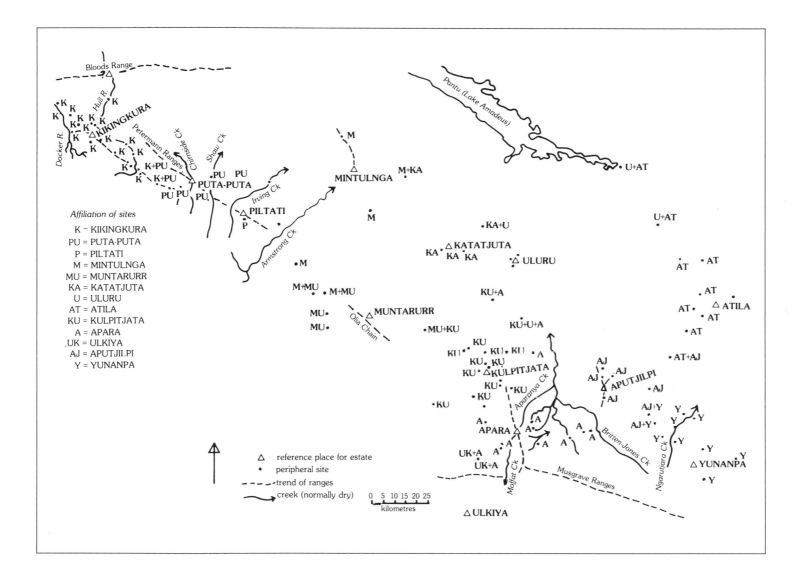

Figure 2
Ownership of places and location of estates.

representatives of both. Mountford recognised that the categories were generational divisions (1977, pp.19 and 96), but he believed that the Rock was divided between two descent groups because he thought the individual's personal dreaming, the one he or she acquires from the 'birth' place, was something inherited from his or her father.

On different occasions, I collected lists of places that Paddy Uluru and Nipper Winmati attributed to the Uluru estate (Table 4). These show without question that both men considered the Rock as a unity (*see* Figure 3).

Table 4 **Places attributed to Uluru estate by Paddy Uluru and Nipper Winmati**

Paddy Uluru's list	*Nipper Winmati's list*
Mutitjulu	Mutitjulu
Kulpi Turrmil (Kulpi Mutitjulu)	Kalaya Tjunta
	Wila Alpuru
Kurumpa	Kuniya Piti
Alyurungu	Taputji
Kapi Yularanya Tjukutjuku (SG52–8 387862)	
Inintitjara	Inintitjara
Tjuku Tjapi	
Kantju	Kantju
Walaritja (collected at Ayers Rock,	
22 November 1977)	Mala Wipu (the climb)
	Walu Kutjuta
	Mutjuranpa (near Walu Kutjuta)
	Lungkata Waru (Mita Kampantja)
	Pularinya
	Patji (SG52-8 405823)
	Kapi Yularanya Pulka (SF52-8 389866)
	Kapi Yularanya Tjukutjuku (collected at Areyonga,
	23 March 1978)

Since the existence of reliable water at a base camp is crucial, estates tend to be focused on the ranges, where there are more rock holes, and more soaks in the otherwise dry beds of the creeks. Nine of the fifteen estates in the Ayers Rock region lie along the chain of hills forming the Petermann and Bloods Ranges, the Olia Chain and the Musgrave Ranges. In the ranges, the centres of estates also lie closer together.

The average area of estates is about 1500 square kilometres, half the average size of the nearest cattle stations. The average population of the group holding the estate is about thirty, implying a traditional population density of about one person per 50 square kilometres. Although low, this is about four times the number of people living in an equivalent area and supported by the region's cattle industry today.

Foraging range

Pitjantjatjara and Yankunjatjara use the term *ngura*, or in English, 'country', to refer to estates, but both *ngura* and 'country' are also used to talk about other kinds of territorial unit. In its most specific sense, a *ngura* is a camp. A base camp is a *ngura pulka* (big camp), a peripheral one a *ngura tjukutjuku* (small camp). The term is also used to describe what W.E.H. Stanner (1965) called a group's foraging range, which was wider than its estate.

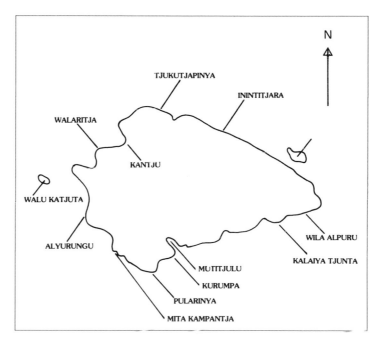

Figure 3
Places at Uluru listed by Paddy Uluru and Nipper Winmati.

A land-owning group's range is referred to as *ngura kaputu*. This expression was first recorded by Nancy Munn in her work with Pitjantjatjara men whose estates lie in the Petermann Ranges (Munn 1965, p.3) and more recently has been obtained by Dan Vachon from Pitjantjatjara men at Indulkana (Vachon, personal communication). In English, people sometimes refer to their group's traditional range as its 'run', comparing it with the movement of cattle on a pastoral station. Figure 4 shows the approximate limits of the foraging range from Uluru and Kikingkura.

To enter neighbouring estates unaccompanied, people had to know the legends and the location of sacred sites in those estates (cf. Tonkinson 1978, p.53). Older men are well-versed in such knowledge, which they develop and express in ceremonies, but at a certain point people would reach 'foreign' country outside their regular range. Unless authorised and accompanied by local people, one would not travel or forage in such an area. This seems to be what some of the Kikingkura men meant when they told Harney they could not stay at Uluru until admitted to local ritual knowledge (Harney 1969, p.53). During court hearings for the land claim on country around Ayers Rock, one local man was asked whether someone from Indulkana could camp at Uluru. His reply was that because the visitor would be embarrassed, the local man would teach him the dreaming (transcript p.612).

Rights and responsibilities of the land-owning group

Each estate contains sections of two or more major ancestral tracks, and each track is associated with a string of sites recording incidents in the ancestors' travels. Song verses, part of the *inma* cycles recording each ancestral saga, relate to these sites. The unity of the estate is seen as something that derives from the sacred sites it holds. At Indulkana, Dan Vachon recorded the phrase *ngura inmanguru*, or 'country from the *inma*', as a specific term for an estate. Some of the major traditional rights and responsibilities of the land-owning group are to maintain and transmit the sacred knowledge belonging to their estate. Such knowledge relates to the collectivity of ancestral beings who entered and shaped the estate. At Uluru, for instance, it includes the Mala and Kuniya; at Atila, the Wati Nyinnga (Ice Men) and Kungarangkalpa ('Seven' Sisters). Thus it is wrong to think of the land-owning group having a single 'totem'. Although some senior men may have particularly profound knowledge of the lore associated with a specific track, the whole group shares responsibility for the total body of knowledge belonging to the estate. When *inma* are performed at collective ceremonies, members of the group start the singing of the verses belonging to their country. It is the group's responsibility to pass this knowledge on to its children and to teach members of neighbouring estates. It is also its responsibility to protect sites to which access is forbidden to women or children, and to prevent revelation of sacred knowledge to the uninitiated. Traditionally, serious offences might result in execution. Paddy Uluru knew of an incident, a few generations ago, when a woman was speared for picking wild figs in a sacred area at the foot of the Rock. If the owners failed to exact punishment, they would themselves be at risk for ignoring their responsibilities. Ritual knowledge is still jealously guarded today, and it continues to provide the core of Aboriginal identity within a living culture. Women have their share of knowledge, which relates to the same ancestral traditions but develops different aspects and events within the narrative and I would like to have been able to learn far more of this.

Children begin to accept their part in the group's responsibility when they are old enough to be initiated. Initiation qualifies them to begin acquiring deeper levels of knowledge, not just in one estate but also in both mother's and father's groups, as well as in estates around that where the child has grown up (cf. Wallace 1977, pp.76 and

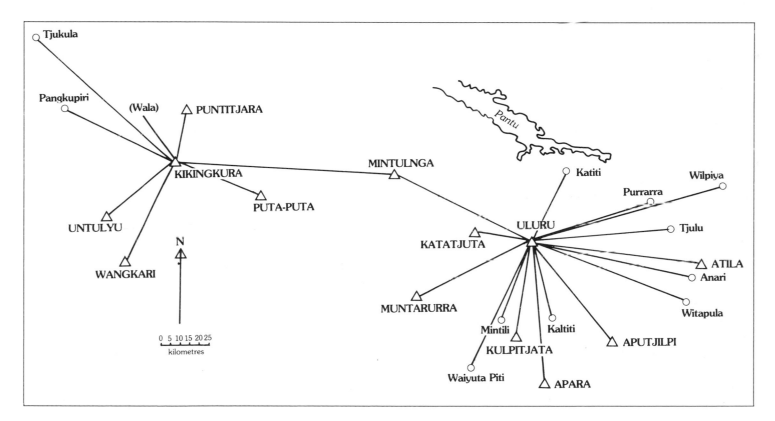

Figure 4

Approximate limits of regular foraging from Uluru and Kikingkura.

78). A Pitjantjatjara or Yankuntjatjara man acquires a progressively wider knowledge of the traditions throughout his area as his seniority grows. During court hearings for the land claim, a number of people spoke of showing their estate to their children, and teaching them its traditions. 'They will come up and they learn the place, and then with their memory that will give them some reason to come and live here . . . you show a person the country, a nice looking place, and they will feel in their hearts that they want to come and live here' (Dan Vachon translating Tjalkalyiri Tiger, transcript p.524). 'The old men bring them [their children] up to love the country; to know the country' (Bill Ukai, transcript p.558). One of the senior women when asked, insisted 'we train the children too' (Mary Tirnpula, transcript p.689).

A man never marries a woman from the same land-owning group as himself. Thus children always begin life with a connection to two estates; their mother's and their father's.

Individual responsibilities to the personal dreaming site

People also have responsibilities to their personal dreaming place—the place where, when they were babies, the stub of their umbilical cord fell off. Each estate contains many places where individual heroes from the creation period left their mark during an episode in the ancestral drama.

Although people are often born in their mother's or father's estate, this is not always the case, and a site's custodian may therefore come from a different land-owning group. It is the custodian's responsibility to clean the site of overgrowing plants and to release its spiritual power by rubbing a boulder or by throwing dust from a soak into the air. People may take over this responsibility on behalf of close relatives who have died, as Paddy Uluru did for his father Lungkata.

The rights of members of neighbouring estates

Shared interests do not arise simply when people are born outside their parents' estates. Because of the way ritual responsibilities are associated with ancestral tracks, the network of tracks breaks down the independence of estates. Each estate draws sections of several tracks into the custodianship of a single group, and each track has the complementary effect of linking a number of estates. Knowledge of tracks extends for considerable distances, and gives members of those estates on the same track a common interest in maintaining the ancestral tradition. The owners of an estate initiate the singing of its songs, and they should attend ceremonies performed in each others' countries and support the singing of their *inma*. Some degree of common interest may be recognised for up to 150 kilometres. People can remember a number of times when the fathers of now senior men settled in their wives' estates and justified this on the grounds that their own and the wife's estate lay on the same ancestral track.

Regular foraging over adjacent estates, and the need for adults so doing to first know the traditions of these neighbouring countries, also breaks down the potential isolation of estates. Members of neighbouring estates will meet and interact at ceremonies, even where they do not share a single ancestral track. Senior men are proud, and acknowledged, to possess an outstanding knowledge of all the *inma* in their area. After Paddy Uluru's death, the task of completing his sons' teaching passed to an Atila man, and at the time of the land claim hearings, it was he who began many of the Mala verses, even though the Mala did not go through Atila country.

Composition of the land-owning group

The typical pattern in Aboriginal Australia is for everyone to inherit membership of their father's land-owning group, but in the Ayers Rock region the group that holds an estate is made up of some people who have inherited membership through their father and some who have inherited membership through their mother. A small percentage join the estate of a more distant relative. At birth, each individual has rights in the land-owning groups of both parents, but during his or her lifetime he or she comes to exercise these rights predominantly in just one group, and it will be membership of this selected group that is transmitted to his or her children.

During the land claim, a member of the group belonging to Aputjilpi was asked why his sister belonged to Apara. He answered that her mother had taken her there and she grew up in Apara (transcript, p.699). If the person is brought up in his or her father's estate, he or she exercises and transmits rights in the father's group; if the person grows up in the mother's estate then it is her group to which the individual is assimilated. Most people do, in fact, join their father's group. In some cases a child joins an estate belonging to a more distant relative, but it is generally adjacent to that of one of his or her parents (see Table 5).

Table 5 **Transmission of membership to land-owning group**

Method of transmission	Number of cases*	Percentage
Through father	79	69
Through mother	23	20
Through more distant relatives		
(a) parent's sibling	9	8
(b) grandparent (not through parent)	3	3
Total	114	100

*Recorded in genealogies collected for land claim.

The flexibility of group membership is illustrated by the following example. The fathers of Pompy Douglas and Pompy Wanampi were two brothers who belonged to Mintulnga, the easternmost Pitjantjatjara estate in the Petermann Ranges, but when they were young men the brothers settled in the Musgrave Ranges, where both married Yankuntjatjara girls—one from Apara and one from Aputjilpi. Pompy Douglas spoke about the marriage of his father to the Apara girl in terms of their dreamings: 'Kalaya (Emu) dreaming been come up, marry him Tjala (Honey Ant) dreaming, honey ant girl'. Emu is the main dreaming for Mintulnga; the track runs through Apara and Kulpitjata country, then along the Olia Chain to Mintul. The two men's fathers were retracing the route of their dreaming when they moved to the Musgraves. Pompy Douglas was born at Wiputa, on the southern margin of Apara country, and Pompy Wanampi at Anari. Both men are considered Yankuntjatjara. 'We're all Yankuntjatjara', said Wanampi, 'never mind my father been Pitjantjatjara, my mother was Yankuntjatjara'. Wanampi described how his father had led other Petermann men into the country around Uluru and, according to Jimmy Walkabout of Kikingkura, only one man had been left at Mintulnga. Imalangu (Harry Bigfoot) suggested that the name for Petermann people, the Pitja-pitja, which means 'come-come' or 'go-go', was derived from so many having left their country

of birth. One man who made a similar move was the father of Peter Bulla, Tjalkalyiri and Napala Jack. His country was Piltati, to the west of Mintulnga. He married two girls, one from Katatjuta, one from Apara.

During hearings for the land claim, many questions were asked of Aboriginal witnesses to try to establish whether it was enough for a person to have inherited rights to membership of a land-owning group through a parent, or whether he had to have taken up those rights to count as a member of the group. It was clear that people recognised a distinction between children who had not returned to the parent's estate and those who had, but the witnesses insisted that even those children who had not returned still had a duty to learn, and the older members of the group, a duty to teach them about the estate. Bill Ukai said that children who go to live elsewhere still think of Katatjuta and Ayers Rock as being their country from their mothers and fathers (transcript, p.557).

The flexibility of such an arrangement would be an advantage in the uncertain desert conditions, and one of the ways it seems to have been applied was to allow a gradual movement of people out from the centre of the Western Desert toward its more hospitable margins. In most of the cases where men joined their mother's group around Uluru, the man's father came from further west. One man's father moved from Untulyu to Kikingkura (see Figure 4 for locations). In another case, a man's father's father moved from Piltati in the Petermann Ranges to his wife's estate, Muntarurra, in the Olia Chain. The man's father moved in turn to his wife's estate in the Musgrave Ranges, and he himself, while claiming membership of both his mother's and father's estates, has been actively involved in ceremonies for his mother's country. In yet another instance, a younger man has chosen to be identified with ritual responsibilities in his mother's estate at Ilturr, south of the Musgrave Ranges, rather than his father's estate, Atila. It was a particular phase in this movement, probably accelerated by drought in the Mann Ranges, that N.B. Tindale described as the 'Pitjantjatjara Invasion' (1959, p.325; 1974, p.212). Both Noel Wallace and I concluded that it was not an invasion, but a steady drift of people along socially defined lines.

Peter Brokensha (1975, pp.10–11) discusses the published evidence for general movement from the centre of the Western Desert. F.G.G. Rose also refers to it, speculating as to whether movement was always away from the centre of the desert or whether it fluctuated according to climatic variations. He argues that European influence would have been felt from the last quarter of the nineteenth century, when the founding of Alice Springs, the building of the overland telegraph, and starting of the railway could have had effects throughout the Centre (1965, pp.6, 13 and 15). If this is the case, then all recorded movements might reflect this impact, but it would not call into question the traditional nature of the system's flexibility.

PART TWO

Conflict and change

CHAPTER 4

Exploration

It is only a hundred years since White people first entered the Ayers Rock region. Occasional early visits did not disrupt the Aboriginal subsistence economy, and between the 1870s and 1930s, explorers and surveyors had an opportunity to record the traditional way of life. Many of the senior people with whom I worked had reached adulthood before the subsistence economy collapsed. During the 1930s contact had intensified, when cattle stations began to encroach from established pastoral areas further north and east, gold prospectors and dingo scalp hunters entered the area, and a severe drought drove the Petermann people from their homeland. By 1940, the traditional pattern of land use was almost destroyed.

Not all Whites who entered the area have left written records. Early explorers, such as W.E.P. Giles, W.C. Gosse and H. Basedow, provided detailed, daily accounts of their contacts. Surveyors such as John Carruthers and Donald Mackay, wrote brief reports. Some popular descriptions, such as those by W. Gill and A. Groom, contain valuable material. Other travellers, like Michael Terry and Errol Coote, avoided close contact with local people, and in their accounts they perpetuate popular prejudice about Aboriginal culture. But many people left no accounts at all. W.E. Harney comments on the irony that anonymous surveyors and the men who traded supplies for dingo scalps were in the area

53

before many of those who dramatised their own pioneering journeys in print (1969, pp. 156 and 169).

Some of those who did publish accounts of their expeditions found the Aboriginal people hostile and failed to make friendly contact. This seems to have most often been the case when they met large groups, and the lack of contact seems to be as much the result of fear on the Whites' part as of Aboriginal aggression. W. Gill recognised this at the time as is seen later in this Chapter.

The earliest explorers gave creeks and hills European names; they did not discover those already used by the Pitjantjatjara and Yankuntjatjara. W.E.P. Giles, between 1872 and 1874, named Mount Olga, Lake Amadeus, the Petermann Ranges, and its hills and creeks. In 1873, W.C. Gosse named Ayers Rock and Mount Conner. While at Uluru, he twice met Aboriginal people also camped there. On 3 August he saw camp fires on its western side and met two young men who came to get water. Gosse learnt that the local word for water was 'carpee' (*kapi*). In the Petermann Ranges during 1874, Giles had several unfriendly encounters with large groups. Once he and his companion W.H. Tietkins were chased by 'a multitude of howling demons'. Spears were thrown and Tietkins fired his revolver. After travelling nine miles, Giles and Tietkins made camp. 'While we were eating our dinner, Mr Tietkins gave the alarm that the enemy was on

us again ... These wretches seemed determined to destroy us, for having considerably augmented their numbers, they swarmed about us on all sides.' Giles and Tietkins drove them off with revolver fire but kept stiff upper lips. Giles recorded that when the party had gone, '...we broke all the spears we could lay our hands on, nearly a hundred, and then finished our dinner' (Giles 1889, vol. 2 pp.7–9). Later his expedition went to Uluru, where they were visited by a small group of three men. Giles comments with surprise, 'They were not only the least offensive and most civil we had met on any of our travels, but they were almost endearing in their welcome to us' (p.65).

Tietkins returned to the region, in charge of his own expedition, in 1889. He kept north of the Petermann Ranges, naming Mount Currie and two prominent hills in the Bloods Range. He saw very little of the local inhabitants, although, turning back on his own tracks near the western end of Lake Amadeus, he found they had been followed by four people (Tietkins 1891, p.51). At the Olgas, he saw several fires close to their own camp, but no one visited them and they did not go to the Aboriginal camp (p.55).

The earliest collection of indigenous place names was made by John Carruthers, who worked in the Musgrave and Mann Ranges between 1888 and 1890 but wrote only a brief report of his field experiences. He learnt that the inhabitants of the Musgraves had already met White people. Ernabella was among the Aboriginal names he recorded.

W. Baldwin Spencer and F.J. Gillen were the next to collect place names; they were the first writers to visit the area with the deliberate aim of documenting Aboriginal culture. Five years after Tietkins' expedition, they followed Gosse's route to Ayers Rock and the Olgas, obtaining the names of two springs near Lake Amadeus. At the Rock they met 'Lungkatitukukana', probably Paddy Uluru's father Lungkata Tjukurrpa.

The record of Aboriginal place names increased considerably during the Wells expedition of 1903 (Basedow 1914). H. Basedow worked mainly in the Musgrave and Mann Ranges, but part of the team, led by F.R. George, made a detour to the Olgas and Ayers Rock. There is no record of what happened on this section of the expedition, but the names Kartutua (Katatjuta) and Oolooroo (Uluru) appear on Basedow's map. The expedition was accompanied to Apara in the Musgrave Ranges by a party of six men, one woman and two children. This group was heard to use the term *waipella* (White fellow) to refer to members of the expedition (Basedow 1914, p.164), and Basedow records evidence of earlier White parties in the area. Appendix B lists the documentation of Aboriginal place names by Basedow and others.

When F.R. George led an expedition in 1905, two members were speared near Docker River, an event that must have reinforced the picture painted of 'the enemy' by Giles (*see* Terry n.d., p.52). George correctly guessed that the two men had trespassed on a sacred site, and that this was the reason for the attack.

The next recorded expedition seems to be that led by D. Mackay in 1926. Basedow was a member of the team, and Mackay compliments Basedow on his success in communicating with Aboriginal groups. The maps of Mackay (1929) and Basedow (in the Australian Archives), and Mackay's report, contain useful information about the size of groups encountered and place names collected (*see* Appendix B and Table 3).

Intensive contact began in about 1930. Mackay returned to conduct aerial surveys, which required the construction of airstrips in 1930 and 1933. The Lasseter expedition was launched, and ended with Lasseter arriving alone in the Petermann Ranges to lose his camels and die at 'Winter's Glen' (Wakupura), while an Aboriginal family was helping him return eastward through the range. Terry was one of many prompted by Lasseter's claims to lead a prospecting expedition into the Petermanns. Bob Buck went to find Lasseter's body and bury it, near Irving Creek. In the following year, 1931, Buck took Gill into the area, a trip Gill recorded in *Petermann Journey*. Other parties looking for Lasseter's Reef are only hinted at in written records. Perhaps because of its obvious interest to White people and perhaps because of its traumatic effect, the story of Lasseter's days on the Hull River is frequently told by Aboriginal people.

Henry Lasseter claimed to know the location of a gold reef west of the Petermann Ranges, and in 1930 he persuaded a group in Sydney to mount an expedition to help him relocate it. The story is told by E. Coote (1934) and I. Idriess (1931). Unfortunately, the team took the wrong route from Haasts Bluff, and after setbacks, Lasseter was abandoned by the rest of his expedition at Ilbilla, west of Haasts Bluff, when he and the leader of the team fell out. Lasseter decided to continue without them and reached the Petermann Ranges, but his two camels escaped while he was making camp, taking most of his supplies with them. The site at which this is said to have occurred is still known to the Docker River Community. Lasseter established an ambivalent relationship with local Aboriginal people, which is hinted at in his letters and fragments of a diary recovered by a search party, and imaginatively reconstructed (partly from this evidence) by Idriess. Lasseter took refuge in a small rockshelter where the Hull River cuts through the Petermann Ranges at Tjunti, where he was brought food and where eventually he buried his diary. The cave, Kulpi Tjuntinya or Lasseter's Cave, is now marked with a commemorative sign board erected by the Docker River Social Club. The portion of the Hull River in the vicinity of this shelter, Karu Kali, is

sometimes also called Latata (Lasseter) Creek.

Leslie Mintjantji, one of the men in whose country Tjunti is situated, described how they returned to their own country after a foraging expedition made after rain and found Lasseter established in their terrain. Jimmy Walkabout (Pungkali), also a senior member of the group, described himself as 'Lasseter's Friend' and said he had helped gather bush food to keep him alive. Lively, or Palingka, C.P. Mountford's main informant at Uluru, was said to have been another of the men in the area at the same time as Lasseter. Lasseter had given Lively a note, asking him to take it to Alice and bring back more flour. Lively refused, asking why Lasseter couldn't live off bush food like everyone else. When Lasseter finally decided to wait no longer and to make his way towards the Olgas in the hope of meeting a rescue party, it was, said Jimmy, the family of his older brother Wintjin who had helped him as far as he could travel before he died near Piltati in the Petermann Ranges. When we visited Lasseter's Cave, Paddy Uluru described how Lasseter had fired his revolver at some of the people who approached while he was camped there, but a *nangkari* (doctor) who had a stone in his chest stood in front, and the bullets, when they struck him, ricocheted away. While this illustrates how the events have become interpreted within a non-European frame of reference, Idriess's account also suffers from a distinct slant towards a particular view of Aboriginal culture. On another occasion, Paddy's son Cassidy, who was too young to have seen Lasseter and therefore repeating what to him must be a traditional narrative, gave me the following account:

> One man, before White men came, came down from Tjitjingati [where the Docker River road now crosses Irving Creek] to Puta-puta, towards Tjunti. His camels ran off; I don't know what happened, maybe the saddlebags slipped [and frightened them]. All his sugar, flour and tea gone. He finished up in the little cave at Tjunti; wrote a letter and gave it to Captain [another of the men in the local group]. He asked him to take it to Henbury Station; that was as far as White men had come down in those days. But Aboriginal people couldn't read, they didn't know what it was. Captain went half way to Katatjuta, then he caught a kangaroo and lost the note and came back. The White man got angry. After a little while he wrote a second letter and gave it to another man, but the same thing happened. When the man came back, Lasseter got really crook; he fired his gun and everyone laid down. But that second man, he was a *nangkari*, a doctor, he had a stone in his chest. When the bullet hit him it just bounced off.

Cassidy's account shows that the early contact period is still significant for younger Aboriginal people. The remains of Lasseter's diary, which Idriess reproduces at the end of his account (1931), seem to record some of the same incidents. One entry reads;

> The old man has just come [to the cave] and pointed the water and bough shelter out to me again saying "capei caro" "capei caro" about one dozen times [*kapi karu* =creek water]. I have given him this book and saying: "Alice Springs" "Alice Springs", 100 times . . . Old fellow returned with despatch book today having failed to get thro' to Alice Springs. He was all played out so I gave him a rabbit I had dug out (p.249) . . . Today I crept out to try and get some green feed and chewed a herb which was poison. Old man with wart very kind young blacks gathered round and laughed fired my 3 last shots and they ran like hell (p.250).

The account that C. Duguid obtained from a man encountered in the Petermann Ranges in 1939 puts the emphasis slightly differently: Lasseter's story, writes Duguid (1972, p.133),

> is well known . . . Tjuintjara added something to the story by telling us that Lasseter crawled into a cave— which he showed us later—and resisted Aboriginal attempts to help him by firing his rifle whenever they approached. When he lapsed into unconsciousness they carried him out and built a rough shelter round him, and sent a messenger to fetch Bob Buck, a settler whose station (Middleton Ponds) was many miles to the east.

Whether Lasseter's gold reef existed, or whether it was a figment of his imagination, has never been established, yet in the following years many explorers believed the legend. Among them was Michael Terry, who put together a well-organised party equipped with a motor vehicle. Terry's contacts with the Aboriginal people were limited. He reflects the attitude of the place and time in his account of Erldunda Station's extension westward towards Mount Conner.

To give some idea how new is the settlement of this extension of this last station on the edge of the untamed black fellow's country, it is interesting that while the Baileys were opening up Pulcarra [an artesian spring 70 kilometres east of Mount Conner] . . . they had to hunt away wild bush blacks or myalls who were becoming a nuisance and hindering the work. (n.d.24).

The imperative brushes aside any question of the Aboriginal people's need for water.

Travelling back through the Petermann Ranges from the Ruined Ramparts, Terry's expedition met what they estimated to be four hundred Aboriginal people assembled for a ceremony (pp.57–9). Given Terry's buccaneering style, this may be an over-estimate. 'Wishing to have as little as possible to do with such a great assembly . . . we drove on without delay'—so fast, in fact, that they abandoned the members of the expedition travelling by camel to make their own way past the gathering (p.58). W.M. Hilliard, however, describes how Terry introduced some of the local people to the motor truck (1968, p.74).

W. Gill and Bob Buck, who went through the range the following year, made much closer contact. They expected to find people at Piltati, one of the traditional base camps where Mackay had met a large group, but it was deserted. Buck thought perhaps there was a fear of retribution for Lasseter's death. The first meeting took place a few miles away, where a group of two men, four women and a youth and 'a gaggle of small children' were found at a camp, waiting for others to return from foraging. 'As a crowd,' Gill comments, 'the first thing to become apparent was their nervousness. Buck kept harping on how treacherous they were' (1968, p.88). Gill questioned him, and concluded, 'he was not fearful in a physical sense. It was just that he was reacting instinctively to a situation which, though not exactly outside his experience, was one that he was finding difficult to appreciate' (p.90). Gill estimated that by nightfall there were thirty-three people in the camp. The whole group walked with them to Lasseter's grave, in Winter's Glen, but then dispersed. Buck, Gill and their party proceeded to the Hull River, where they found one hundred and thirty people preparing for a ceremony (p.110). Despite frequent misgivings at being outnumbered and unsure of the other side's intentions, Buck and Gill accepted an invitation to watch. Gill did finally encounter antagonism when he attempted to photograph a fight.

Mackay's aerial surveys are described by F. Clune (1942). The 1933 expedition, which penetrated the Petermann Ranges, required the construction of an airstrip at Docker River. Bob Buck was chosen to go ahead of the survey team and construct the strip, which he did using Aboriginal labour. This is of particular interest, because Paddy Uluru pointed out to me a site in the Petermanns where he had helped construct an airstrip: the site was adjacent to a hill called Mulya

Ngatara (SG52–7 255874), between Chirnside and Shaw Creeks. Paddy Uluru said that fuel for the planes was brought by camel from Henbury Station, while the planes themselves flew from Hermannsburg:

We been cut him all that tree, see him that aeroplane. Two aeroplane come this way from the mission, Hermannsburg, land there. We been burn him then all the bush: winter time, you know, no wind [i.e., it was all right to fire the bush]. 'Why you been burn him?' [people asked]. Well, you'll see. All the fellows don't know, all the natives. You see him, he coming all right, two aeroplanes. A big mob [of camels] get him petrol, *big* mob. 'Were there people here, then?' All there, big mob, I been see them, all the [since] dead fellows.

Clune tells the story from the White point of view, but it is one that bears comparison with Paddy Uluru's. Perhaps because a ceremony was being held at Docker River, Buck was told by the local people that he would find little water in that area. He decided instead to establish camp on Chirnside Creek. The decision was relayed to Alice by radio.

The expedition left Alice Springs in the afternoon of 25 May (1933), and reached Hermannsburg Mission an hour later ... On 28 May, the explorers flew in company in a south-westerly direction ... A hundred miles west of Mount Olga, Bob Buck's smoke signal ascended in the air like a beckoning finger.
  At midday both planes were safely grounded on the new aerodrome Buck had prepared at Chirnside Creek. The new arrivals were greeted by the casual but capable Bob, Lovell the wireless operator, and Dutchy the cook. From a safe distance a hundred wild natives of the Petermanns watched in awe as the machines landed. (Clune 1942, pp.271–2)

Mackay calculated that Chirnside Creek lay just beyond the aeroplane's range from the next survey base in the Pilbara. He insisted that Buck proceed to Docker River, to construct the strip where it had originally been planned. There turned out to be plenty of water, but Clune apparently failed to appreciate that he might be interfering in the ceremony (*see* Clune 1942, pp.272 and 278).

The 1930s were fateful for the people of the Petermann Ranges. A severe drought provoked movement out of the area, and many people migrated south-eastwards. There is good evidence that similar droughts must have occurred in the past. The 'Pitjantjatjara Invasion' of which N.B. Tindale writes (*see* Chapter 3), which involved the movement of groups out of the Mann Ranges— south of the Petermanns—east into the Musgrave Ranges, took place twenty years earlier.

The difference now was that people moving south or east encountered White settlement advancing from the opposite direction. Reliable hunting and gathering was no longer possible, and people were instead confronted with inescapable dependence on the White economy. Tindale is probably correct in saying that the relative security the latter offered, at a time of drought, may actually have encouraged people to move toward White settlements, but it was also bound up with apparently traditional behaviour.

By the end of the 1930s, much of the Petermann Ranges' population had left, drawn into the cattle station or mission economies. In 1939, T.G.H. Strehlow was asked to lead an expedition to find out why so many people were moving to stations many miles east of their own country. Strehlow invited C. Duguid to go with him, rightly considering the trip too risky to undertake with only one truck (Duguid 1972, p.131). At Piltati, they met a man called Tjuintjara sitting with his son at the waterhole. He showed them Lasseter's grave and described the events leading to Lasseter's death. Tjuintjara also explained that there had been a long drought in the Petermanns, causing many people to die. Some of the survivors had decided it was better to leave their tribal territory (p.133).

Travelling on to the Docker River, Strehlow and Duguid met a group who told them they had sold dingo scalps to White doggers who had been in the area without government permission (p.134). On the entire trip through the Petermann Ranges, they met only twenty-six people, all of whom were forced by the lack of food and water to travel in small groups. There were no large ceremonies of the sort seen by Gill or Mackay at the start of the decade; people told them it had been impossible to hold a ceremony for three years. They themselves saw no kangaroo, euro, wallaby or emu during their journey (p.135). The journey is also described in Duguid (1963, pp.55–69). It is clear that the movement towards White settlement was not brought about simply by the alleged attractions of settlement.

CHAPTER 5

Europe
use of land

Pastoralism

It is easy to overlook how recently White contact disrupted the traditional way of life among Aboriginal cultures in central Australia. After the telegraph station had been established in 1872, the first pastoral properties grew up around Alice Springs, appropriating portions of Aranda and Luritja country. Erldunda, Henbury, Glen Helen and Tempe Downs were among the earliest properties established, dating between 1870 and 1900. Henbury was established before 1877 and Tempe Downs leased and stocked in 1885 (Duncan 1967, p.162).

As the inroads made by White settlement intensified, so, frequently, did Aboriginal resistance. Erldunda homestead was attacked in 1887 (Hartwig 1965, pp.401 and 419). Pastoralism had a dramatic effect on the natural resources vital to the Aboriginal subsistence economy. Before 1924, the Crown Lands Ordinance of the Northern Territory did not reserve any rights on pastoral land for the Aboriginal inhabitants. After that date, leases were issued that allowed Aboriginal people entry onto pastoral leases, to use springs and natural surface water, to hunt wild animals, and to erect traditional camps. Unfortunately these rights were largely undermined by the effect pastoralism had on the country. Major water sources were tapped with bores and tanks while soaks and rock holes became rapidly polluted by wandering stock. Both people and the animals they hunted suffered, as many species of food animal became extinct (*see* Frith 1973 and 1978). Pointing out that traditionally it was the small and more easily caught animals which provided most of the meat, H.J. Frith writes that it was these which suffered most from grazing. In the 1930s, H.H. Finlayson established that central Australia had twenty-nine species of marsupial and eight types of rodent. By 1970, fourteen species, including most of the bandicoots and small wallabies, were extinct. Frith concludes that it would probably now be impossible for small native mammals to provide a substantial part of Aboriginal people's diet. They have succumbed both to the changes made to their plant environment and to exotic predators, such as cats and foxes (Frith 1978, p.90). Even more severe was the effect that grazing stock had on the plants that provided Aboriginal people with the greater part of their diet. G.M. Chippendale (1963) found that one year after cattle were pastured on previously ungrazed land in central Australia, the quantity and diversity of vegetation fell by *two-thirds*, but even then it was *ten times* higher than that available on land that had been grazed for many years. Frith, who quotes these figures, points out that they were obtained during drought, but records that when rain later fell, the vegetation did not recover its original diversity or abundance (Frith 1978, p.89).

It was often drought that precipitated violence. The Alyawara people first came into contact with pastoralism in 1888, but during a severe drought that afflicted their country in 1895–96, they speared and killed 600 cattle that had wandered into the hills where the local people were camped (Hagen and Rowell 1978, p.14). Combined with attacks on homesteads, such incidents forced the early settlers to withdraw. The core of Alyawara country was not settled until after the Second World War (Hagen & Rowell 1978, pp.13 and 19). Coniston Station, established in 1917, was the first property set up on Warlpiri land (Peterson, Hagen & Rowell, 1978 p.11). During the latter half of the 1920s, drought afflicted the region. The ensuing conflict between Black and White culminated in the Coniston Massacre of 1928, an event that had enormous reverberations through Aboriginal communities north of Alice (*see* Peterson et al. 1978). Fear drove people many miles from their homeland.

According to F.G.G. Rose (1965, p.24), completion of the railway line to Alice Springs brought about a six-fold increase in livestock in central Australia between 1930 and 1950. After 1930, pastoral settlement pushed westward into the Ayers Rock region. Ernabella, when it was established in 1933, became the first station in Yankuntjatjara country. Other properties extended from Erldunda to Mount Conner and it was toward these that the people of the Petermann

Ranges found themselves pushed by the drought of the late 1930s.

Dick Kimber argued in his evidence to the Uluru land claim hearing that the Yankuntjatjara had traditional rights of access to Luritja country around Tempe Downs during drought. He refers to evidence that it was common practice among early pastoralists between northern South Australia and the MacDonnell Ranges to discourage Aboriginal people from leaving the homestead area once they had moved onto a station, for fear of disturbing cattle, either by firing the bush or spearing animals for food in lieu of the displaced native species. Kimber cites a pioneer settler who told him that on some properties White people forcibly brought back, or hunted down, anyone who tried to leave their station. He adds, however, that at Henbury and Middleton Ponds, at least, Aboriginal people were better treated (transcript of evidence for Ayers Rock land claim, pp.783–4). The process of persuading people to forgo their traditional life was a long one. As late as the 1950s and 1960s, Pintupi, who until then had managed to preserve their traditional economy, were finally forced by a combination of drought and government pressure to settle at Papunya (see Myers 1976; and Kimber, transcript pp.779–80).

Probably the most fundamental difference between Aboriginal and White exploitation of the land is that while one group obtained all its needs locally, the latter has always been part of a wider system, extracting what resources it can from the bush and exporting them in exchange for what it cannot produce locally. The first attempt to produce an exportable commodity (other than minerals) was based on sheep whose wool could be transported south. Horses were bred for export to India, until the Indian army no longer needed them (see Strehlow 1969a, pp.75 and 81). Beef cattle have since been the basis of the region's pastoral economy.

Sheep-raising failed partly because of dingo attacks on lambs. An important consequence was the promotion of dingo killing, which was encouraged with a government bounty of seven shillings and sixpence on each dingo scalp. White entrepreneurs, known as doggers, drew Aboriginal labour into the alien economy by bartering consumer goods for scalps and profiting by the difference between the cost of these goods and the reward. Employment on pastoral stations also brought Aboriginal people into the White economy, where ration hand-outs provided an imported substitute for the devastated natural food resources. Pompy Douglas, a senior member of the Apara group, described his life on cattle stations. Pompy grew up around Apara and Kulpitjata, but when he was an adolescent, the local group left its own country and moved to Oodnadatta, then the railhead from Adelaide. At Oodnadatta, Pompy met Whites and Afghans for the first time, and learnt to speak English and how to drive camels. For most of his adult life he worked on cattle stations, receiving rations but no pay. His old age pension, he thought, was a poor reward for those years.

At the time central Australia was being colonised exponents of pastoral development saw vast, untapped resources, but its critics anticipated the despoilation that tapping these resources would cause. The two sides of the argument are represented in the views of T.E. Day and Pastor Albrecht (senior). Day was sent to report on the prospect of the country west of the overland telegraph line, and his findings were published as a Northern Territory Bulletin in 1916. He responded ecstatically to what he saw as the region's prospects for mineral and pastoral exploitation. To avoid falling behind the other States in the race for economic development, he claimed, South Australia 'must attract both [capital and population] by offering a liberal share in the dormant wealth lying about in almost criminal uselessness now' (Day 1916, p.6). Day, however, recognised the effect that stock were having on the region's vegetation. He describes conditions at Goyder Springs, a series of artesian springs on the edge of a salt lake, near Erldunda. At the principal spring a bore casing had been put down to about 24 metres, supplying water to cattle troughs. The surrounding country, he wrote: 'shows evidence of very heavy stocking. I understand a thousand head of cattle get water here, the mulga and edible shrubs being nearly all eaten out' (p.13). Even Day considered the country west of Mount Conner and south of Lake Amadeus to be of no value for pastoralism, but he thought well of the MacDonnell Ranges. He shows the importance of Aboriginal labour when he comments that:

> On many of the larger holdings the lessees are able to graze a fair number of stock on natural waters, and by employment of Aboriginal labour only; if better watering facilities were provided ... the stock-carrying capacity of the stations would be greatly increased, with the consequent employment of additional White labour. (p.17)

Implicit in this view is the fact that it cost more to hire White labour. In a report to the government published in 1919, Baldwin Spencer (1919, p.12) wrote uncompromisingly about the part played by Aboriginal people on cattle stations:

> While it is true that in some parts the Aboriginal gives trouble, it is equally true that, at the present day, practically all the cattle stations depend on their labour and, in fact, could not get on without it, any more than the police constables could. They do work that it would be very difficult to get White men to do and do it not only cheerfully but for a remuneration that in many cases, makes all the difference at the present time between working the cattle station at a profit or a loss.

The impact of pastoralism on traditional subsistence was portrayed by Albrecht, writing from Hermannsburg Mission in 1937. After grazing licences had been issued in the Haasts Bluff area, he protested:

> This great area the source of food to such a considerable number of natives may not be taken from them for the benefit of one White man ... The waterholes there are only in limited numbers, and these will be used for sheep, and therefore no longer accessible to natives. Berries, grass seeds, etc., the stand by for natives will be eaten by the sheep. The natives ... driven to desperation in the quest for food, are bound to interfere with the flocks, with the result that the heads of families, and groups will be brought into the Alice Springs jail ... As has been demonstrated on most parts of the settled area of Central Australia, the country does not improve but suffers through being stocked, and after a number of years, practically all the bush-tucker is destroyed.

Albrecht estimated the Aboriginal population of the Haasts Bluff area to be between 200 and 250 (AA1). T.G.H. Strehlow and C. Duguid made similar objections, and the lessees' grazing licences were withdrawn, after which Hermannsburg Mission took over administration of the Haasts Bluff area.

In the earliest years of contact, settlers received the tacit support of the government when they took it into their own hands to discourage or punish cattle-killing by Aboriginal people, and the evidence suggests that most police officers saw it as their duty to protect Europeans against Aborigines rather than both equally (Hartwig 1965, p.420). In 1878, Northern Territory police were instructed not to resort to severe measures, except in the last extremity or in self-defence, or where there was 'fair evidence that the natives belonged to the tribe criminally concerned in the outrages'.

The 'tribe' is an ill-defined and rather large group to hold collectively responsible for cattle spearings or even the killing of a White man. Notwithstanding this, when the police instructions were passed to the Attorney-General he concluded that they were the best that could be given in the circumstances, justifying himself with the comment:

> It is in my opinion utterly out of the question to suppose that we can deal with the natives in the Northern Territory as if they were civilised. I think that the case is hardly one of law but essentially one of policy. (Hartwig 1965, p.421)

As a result of this policy, it was not uncommon for Aboriginal people to be shot, flogged or otherwise mistreated without recourse to the law. M.C. Hartwig points out that there were two convenient excuses offered by the law to those who shot Aboriginal people: that they had shot in self-defence or, if they were police or special constables, that the victim had been shot while resisting arrest. Although Aboriginal evidence carried, in theory, equal weight to that of European witnesses in court, nothing was done to ensure that impartiality was observed. Sometimes, particularly from the 1880s onwards, police officers were pressed to explain why they had shot an Aboriginal person, but no inquest was ever held and, with one exception, there was no attempt made to corroborate the police witness's account from Aboriginal evidence. Only once did a policeman go on trial, when Constable Willshire was tried after two Aboriginal men were shot at Tempe Downs in 1891 and, on his instructions, their bodies burnt. Although damaging evidence was given by several Aboriginal witnesses, Willshire was acquitted (Hartwig 1965, p.431–3).

Even in 1943, Mackay was able to write in a report (1943, pp.4–5) on central Australia:

> Of the Australian Aborigine who inhabits the far distant land mentioned in this report we hear little until a startling headline in the press draws our attention to the fact that some luckless prospector has been speared while on a quest for gold. Too often it is taken for granted that the native is at fault and vituperative expressions such as 'treacherous', 'savage', 'bloodthirsty' etc. are used before the facts are known. Excited ignorant people demand a punitive expedition with the result that scores of innocent native human beings are killed in reprisal for the death of one man who, by his want of knowledge of native customs or his reckless disregard of them may have brought his death upon himself.

The defence that someone had been shot because it was impossible to capture them appears to have been relied upon by the police constable involved in an incident at Uluru during 1934. This event has been documented in official records for the period (see AA19 and AA20), but there is another shooting still well-remembered by local people, which apparently went unnoticed by the authorities. It is said that at some point during the early 1930s, a group of Aboriginal men were rounded up in the Tempe Downs–Middleton Ponds area after they had speared goats belonging to a station. The men were set to work digging a hole they were told was a well, but an Aboriginal girl living with the White man revealed that it was their own grave they were digging. Her warning proved to be true. As soon as the Whites began shooting, one man threw himself to the ground and was later able to escape from among the bodies of his companions.

M. Terry wrote of the need to drive away 'wild bush blacks' who were making a nuisance of themselves at a natural well being taken over for cattle at Erldunda. During the 1930s, Lyndavale homestead, which drew its water from Marutjara, was built by W.L. ('Snowy') Pearce. He took up a pastoral lease on surrounding country, which until then had been used by Erldunda. Paddy Uluru said he had been working with 'Snowy' Pearce near Marutjara when asked to go to the Petermann Ranges to help construct the airstrip at Mulya Ngatara, in 1933. C.P. Mountford collected one of the men he took to Uluru in 1940 from Pearce's homestead (1950, pp.70 and 73). Later, part of Pearce's lease was reincorporated into Erldunda, and the homestead is now abandoned.

In 1947, when they were travelling between Mount Conner and Angas Downs, Tjalkalyiri told A. Groom, 'Long time ago this country belong to Bill Liddle and Snow Pearce—they have plenty sheepee [sic] but pappy-dawg eat sheepee and native shepherd lose too many. All cattle country now' (Groom 1950, p.191).

Patrick de Conlay established a homestead at Anari in 1943 and started Mount Conner station. Toby Nangina told me that it was he who showed 'Paddy Connally' the location of Anari, although the site was already known to some Whites (*see* Appendix B). Groom gives a graphic description of the de Conlays' isolation—from a White perspective—when he visited the homestead in 1947. Only Mrs de Conlay was at home. Groom describes the homestead: a single-roomed hut, which seemed to serve as living room, kitchen, store, office and harness room. Some Aboriginal women and children moved about indoors while others looked on from outside. The room was stuffy and packed with stores, tables, cases of food, a meat safe, a bed curtained off from the rest of the room, and a sewing machine. Groom was offered some beef, and Mrs de Conlay explained:

> Got a killer in a couple of days ago. Had to. Natives on walkabout hopped in and pinched most of what I had the week before. Poor beggars. They go walkabout from station to station, and you feel you *must* give them some sort of a handout. (1950, p.186)

Punch Thomson, one of the present members of the Atila Estate, was born near the de Conlays' homestead in 1946.

Two years before de Conlay established his station at Mount Conner, Mervin Andrews founded Curtin Springs. Tjuki, a man born in Luritja country, described the circumstances. Andrews, he said, had formerly been a partner in a station near Ulannga (Olunga Well, south of Wallara Ranch): 'old wurly there [a bough shade] ... sort of a station', was how Tjuki characterised it. When the water at Olunga failed during drought, Andrews and his Aboriginal stockmen set out to look for a new source, travelling south past Mutata, in the Liddle Hills and Wilpiya (Wilbia Bore) to Iyarrka, where Tjuwirri Harry Brumby knew of water, probably from having camped there as a young man. Tjuwirri showed Andrews where to dig, and when the sand was shovelled away, clear water flowed out. Thus the first homestead was established at Iyarrka or 'Spring Well'. Having found the water, the party returned to Ulannga to muster and brand cattle and load belongings onto wagons. 'No motor car, you know', said Tjuki, 'big mob of wagons and camel, eight camel or six camel or four horse for a wagon'. The stock—bullocks, goats and sheep— were driven south, then around the north side of the Kernot Range. One night they camped at a claypan, another at Ininti, near the site of Inindia Bore. Here, they had to fell trees to clear a road through the scrub for the wagons.

According to Peter Severin, the station's present owner, Andrews found the water at Iyarrka to be too brackish and so later moved his homestead to Tjulu, its present location, after Aboriginal people had also shown him this water. Harney describes Andrews breaking through the limestone wall of the natural well at 'Djulu', 'finding himself waist-deep in cool fresh water' (1969, p.63). Andrews extended pastoral settlement to the shore of Lake Amadeus itself, fitting a hand-pump at the spring called Katiti (Bobbie's Well). Leslie Mintjanti, a younger countryman of Tjuwirri, told me he worked here with Andrews. Andrews timbered the Aboriginal well at Purrarra and deepened it for stock. In drought, Curtin Springs cattle have penetrated as far as Uluru. The Severins took over Curtin Springs from Andrews in 1957, shortly after Harney began work as ranger at the Rock.

Despite the contribution Aboriginal people made to the development of pastoralism in the Centre, life on stations was by no means always pleasant, as was demonstrated in 1941 by the trial of two White men for the murder of an Aboriginal man on Mount Cavenagh station, near Kulgera. The station owner and his White employee maintained that the man had not died, but admitted some of the accusations made by other Aboriginal people who were at the homestead at the time of his alleged murder. The man had been suspected of 'pilfering' from the homestead stores.

The two Whites went to the Aboriginal camp and searched his ration bags, where they thought they found evidence of the theft. During the ensuing argument the man reached for his spears. The accused struck him with a revolver and a rifle, and when the man refused to get up, they put a wire around his neck, tied the other end to the back of a truck and drove to the homestead. Constable Frank McKinnon, the policeman who investigated the allegations, wrote: 'I satisfied myself by conversation with Frank [a witness], that he alleged that after the wire was fastened around Lollylegs' neck he was forced to run behind the moving motor car and fell and was dragged a considerable portion of the 600 yards' (AA2). Accounts differed as to whether the victim had died shortly after, or escaped the following night. McKinnon exhumed a body, which the Aboriginal witnesses told him was that of the dead man, and removed the head. Later, however, this head was identified on medical evidence as that of a young girl, and said to show no sign of injury.

T.G.H Stehlow was one of the first two patrol officers appointed, in the early 1940s, to verify the conditions under which Aboriginal people were employed on cattle stations. On the strength of the admitted treatment of the Mount Cavenagh victim, Strehlow arranged for the withdrawal of the owner's licence to employ Aboriginal people. The latter protested that his action had been justified by the need to be 'firm with Aboriginals', and wrote to the Administrator in Alice Springs (correctly or otherwise), that 'you are no doubt aware ... of how closely my actions followed the usual police methods'. Duguid refers to this case (1963, pp.75–7).

According to E.P. Milliken (1971), regulations governing Aboriginal employment in the pastoral industry were not introduced until 1949. In the same year the government finally agreed to refund pastoralists for the food and clothing they provided to Aboriginal people resident on the stations but not employed (1971, p.90). During the 1960s, Welfare Branch patrol officers played an important part in attempting to control movement of Aboriginal groups through pastoral properties along the boundary of White settlement east of Uluru.

Doggers

For those people who stayed outside the area of pastoral settlement, doggers probably provided the main contact with White culture. Early doggers were an elusive group, living on the margins of White and Aboriginal society, of whom there is little record. W.M. Hilliard has compiled some useful material on doggers in the Ernabella area during the 1930s. All but one of the first pastoral leases taken up in that district were, she writes, primarily dogging camps rather than sheep runs. The men had arrived during the Depression with little or no capital, and they relied on selling dingo scalps to earn an income. Much of the actual hunting was done by Aboriginal people, as was the shepherding of sheep, with the doggers acting more as mediators between the indigenous and White economies (see Hilliard 1968, pp.81, 83 and 96). In 1937, J.R.B. Love visited the North West Reserve, the boundary of which lies not far from Ernabella, to choose a site for a mission. He reported that:

> There are well-defined tracks, of camels and motor cars, left by 'doggers' and prospectors right through the Reserves. Some of these intruders have permits; most have not. The 'Dogging' business is a well organised trade. 'Doggers' ... have their recognised rounds, meeting the natives at the camps and purchasing the scalps off them in the Reserves. The goods used in the trade include flour, tea, sugar, tobacco, matches, shirts and trousers and dresses.
>
> The question whether the natives ought to be clothed has been partly, and unfavourably, decided by doggers ... The doggers argue, justly, that they are giving the natives pay, in their own country, for what is otherwise worthless to them, viz:- for dog scalps. The rate of trade is probably fair as a mere business proposition; no more exacting than the usual country store profits. (Love & Balfour 1937, p.10)

In the winter of 1934, Robert Hughes, a man employed by Pearce at Lyndavale Station, was collecting dingo scalps in the Mount Conner area. He was camped south of Atila, about 3 kilometres from the spring called Anari. With him was Numberlin, an Aboriginal man employed by

Pearce, whose own country was Atila. Around 500 metres away was an Aboriginal camp containing between eighty and ninety people. By 11 August, when he had not eaten meat for several days, Hughes saw kangaroo tracks. A party of five Aborigines, including a young man from Katatjuta called Kai-Umen, his wife 'Judy', and a Petermann Ranges man named Nangee, had just come into Hughes's camp to exchange dingo scalps for rations. Hughes agreed to lend Numberlin, Nangee and Kai-Umen his .22 rifle and two cartridges, so that they could go hunting. Only Numberlin and Nangee returned, with one cartridge and no kangaroo. Hughes asked what had happened to Kai-Umen. Numberlin replied that he was tracking a dingo, the answer he also gave to Judy when she asked about her husband. Hughes told Judy to look for the missing man. According to the evidence Judy later gave in court, she found the hunting party's tracks heading north from Anari to Eraka (Iyarrka) but failed to locate her husband. She returned for the night and the following day (13 August) searched again with the help of two other people from the Aboriginal camp. This time they found Kai-Umen's body. The only other tracks nearby were those of Numberlin and Nangee. Judy dug a hole and buried the body. Meanwhile, Hughes had been up to Iyarrka and returning that day met Jack Anderson, another White dogger. Hughes asked Anderson if he had seen Kai-Umen, to which Anderson replied that

the Aboriginal people were saying Numberlin had killed him. On hearing this, Hughes later reported, he 'got the wind up' at being on his own with so many Aborigines and travelled with Anderson to Ernabella station, where they reported the murder to the police.

Constable McKinnon, who later investigated the Mount Cavenagh case, had left Alice Springs on patrol on 29 July. Learning of the events at Atila, he went to Lyndavale and on 1 September arrested Numberlin. At the inquest, McKinnon's Aboriginal tracker described how Numberlin had denied the charge until McKinnon caught him by the shoulder pushed him down and gave him 'just a little knock with his foot, not very hard'. Having admitted his involvement, Numberlin implicated four others. McKinnon took his prisoner and went to Anderson's camp at Koketera Well, where he arrested the four, including Paddy Uluru. Paddy Uluru said that seven men had been responsible for the killing. These included Numberlin, Nangee and a man named Cowarie. His statement agrees well with Numberlin's and with those all the arrested men made when they were taken by McKinnon to the spot where Kai-Umen had died. He had been killed for revealing secrets to White men, according to Uluru. No mention was made of the rifle; sticks and stones were the only weapons named.

McKinnon took the five men and went to Ilanula, a rocky ridge west of Mount Conner which is a favourite spot for hunting euro. Here they saw Kai-Umen's body covered with mulga branches and stones. McKinnon took the head, which he found 'in a mummified condition'. It was now 30 September, seven weeks after the death. McKinnon's tracker said that by then all tracks around the body had been washed away. Every man, however, continued to admit his involvement, saying they had travelled to the site in two parties.

The police constable took them north to Middleton Ponds. A week later, while he was examining Kai-Umen's skull, he heard something rattle inside. He shook the skull, and a .22 bullet fell out. When this was shown to the prisoners, Numberlin admitted Nangee had used the rifle. Harney (1969, p.40) describes how he was told about this moment twenty-five years later by a man at Angas Downs:

> He told me about the digging up of the body of the murdered man. How the policeman nonchalantly shook the skull and, hearing a rattle inside it, found the man had been killed by a rifle bullet in the head. From tribal business it now became murder, so he chained the culprits to a large tree.

In his evidence, McKinnon describes scraping away dried flesh after he had found the bullet and seeing three wounds in the skull, two from a bullet passing through and one from the bullet that became lodged inside. He also noticed a fracture where the skull had been hit with a stick or stone.

That night, his prisoners escaped. McKinnon caught up with Numberlin four days later and re-arrested him. Numberlin now admitted that he too had shot Kai-Umen with Hughes' rifle. After a further two days' chase, McKinnon describes laconically how he 'tried to re-arrest' another of the men, who 'died as a result of a bullet that was fired'. Harney again relates the story as it was told him at Angas Downs. The escaping prisoners had been on foot, while McKinnon and his tracker pursued them with camels. When they reached Uluru, the men could go no further and hid in a crevice behind the severed nose of the Liru warrior at Mutitjulu. They could hear McKinnon climbing toward them and, eventually, the sound of footsteps creeping into their hiding place. One man, a brother of Paddy Uluru, was too large to squeeze further into the crack. In desperation, he took a stone in one hand and jumped out, hoping to create enough surprise to escape. He was unlucky. McKinnon's rifle mortally wounded him. 'Then,' reports Harney, 'a strange thing happened. The dying man with a superhuman effort, crawled out of the cave and neither threats nor promises could make him reveal where the others were hidden' (1969, p.41).

McKinnon returned to Middleton Ponds with Numberlin. Now Cowarie arrived. This was McKinnon's first encounter with the man the others had named in their statements. He obtained a confession, which Cowarie later withdrew, claiming 'I told McKinnon that I killed that man to get out of getting a hiding. I had to own up because he was giving me too much hiding with a bullock hide.' In his evidence, Cowarie claimed to have heard Numberlin and Nangee admit their responsibility and added the significant statement that Kai-Umen had really been executed for revealing ritual secrets to his wife, Judy.

A fortnight later, McKinnon finally caught Nangee, whom he also arrested. Nangee admitted Kai-Umen had been executed for revealing ritual secrets to his wife. He described how the two parties had jointly carried out the execution, striking Kai-Umen with sticks and stones after they had shot him. Numberlin, Nangee and Cowarie were taken to Alice where an inquest was held. The two men who had used the dogger's rifle were committed for trial while Cowarie was granted immunity from prosecution to give evidence against them. Paddy Uluru left the area and, although he took his family back to Uluru for visits, did not return to live there until he was an old man.

T.G.H. Strehlow has published a brief account of the incident (1970, pp.120–1), in which he states that the local Pitjantjatjara elders ruled Kai-Umen should be executed after they heard the accusation that he had revealed ritual secrets. According to Strehlow, although contrary to the records of the inquest, Kai-Umen's country was Kalaiamurba, north of Piltati (Kaliya Murrpu is another name for Mintulnga). Strehlow records that Nambala (Numberlin) and Nangee were both sentenced to ten years' imprisonment, because the White jury was concerned that a dogger's rifle had been used rather than traditional weapons. Elsewhere (1969b, p.15) Strehlow has published a photograph of members of a Commonwealth Board of Inquiry inspecting the site at Mutitjulu where the escaping man had been shot.

Aboriginal reserves

After his participation in the Wells expedition of 1903, H. Basedow wrote to the Federal Government to suggest establishing a reserve in the south-west corner of the Northern Territory. He visualised an area that would include parts of South and Western Australia and take in the Petermann and Musgrave Ranges. His proposal was rejected on the grounds that it had been insufficiently thought out, but he was supported by the Australian Methodist Conference, who were asked by the Government to set out their plans in more detail. Although Basedow's plan corresponded roughly to the region that eventually became the Petermann, North West and Central Australian Reserves, it appears that for a time no action was taken (AA3).

Baldwin Spencer later advised the Northern Territory administration that reserves were the only appropriate policy 'if the Aborigines are to be preserved and if any serious effort is to be made for their betterment' (cited in the Northern Territory Administration Report for 1920, p.19), and during 1920 an area including the Petermann Ranges and what is now the Uluru National Park was gazetted as an Aboriginal Reserve (Northern Territory Government Gazette, 27 March 1920). During the period when assimilation to European–Australian society was the object of government policy, it was possible to suppose that reserves could be

> ...regarded as refuges or sanctuaries of a temporary nature. The Aboriginal may here continue his normal existence until the time is ripe for his further development. (Northern Territory Annual Report 1938, p.22)

No base was established within the Petermann Reserve to administer the needs of its Aboriginal population, but in 1936 Strehlow argued that a government ration station should be set up. People had already begun to leave, attracted (Strehlow argued) by the European goods doggers had to offer in the area further east, along the margin of pastoral settlement. At least one Petermann Ranges man was implicated in the execution of Kai-Umen. Strehlow proposed a base camp staffed by three officers equipped with two-way radio, and a series of unmanned depots near permanent water sources, which would be regularly visited to collect 'dingo scalps, furs,

native weapons and implements, etc., which would be purchased and paid for with rations' (AA4). The attraction of the exotic goods that doggers had to exchange was not the only incentive to leave, because Strehlow refers to the onset of the drought whose effects he returned to investigate in 1939: 'the life of the Aboriginal within the Reserve has become very arduous by reason of failure of waters and shortage of game' he wrote, and Cook commented:

> It must be admitted that in years gone by Aboriginals were happy in this reserve under the conditions prevailing there and have only recently been attracted to White settlement nearby. It would appear logical to assume that some very serious environmental change has taken place within the reserve. (AA4)

In support of his conclusion Cook cites rainfall figures from Hermannsburg, writing that before 1926 the annual average was 1200 points (305mm). During the next decade, the figures were as follows:

Year	1926	1927	1928	1929	1930	1931	1932	1933	1934	1935	1936
Rainfall (mm)	184	121	66	92	330	152	221	197	177	148	147

Strehlow was against creating ration stations outside the Reserve. He argued this would cause more people to leave. In December of 1936, however, Ernabella Station, a short distance outside the South Australian section of the Reserve, was bought by the Presbyterian Church of Australia to form a mission (Hilliard 1968, pp.95–6). Love and Balfour, investigating possible sites for a mission, considered siting it inside the Reserve, at Apara. Apara had become a trading point for doggers, but Love and Balfour thought that there would not be enough water to support a settled population and, more importantly, Ernabella could be a commercial enterprise. 'A mission station', they wrote in their report 'must have an industry, to provide work and help finance the cost of caring for the natives' (1937, p.5). When the station was taken over, it held 1950 sheep (Hilliard 1968, p.96). In 1948, spinning, dying and weaving wool provided the foundation of a successful craft industry, which also encouraged the manufacture of traditional artefacts for sale and led to a unique style of animal carving. The craft work is documented by W.M. Hilliard (1968) and by P. Brokensha (1975 especially pp.69–9).

T.G.H Strehlow returned from his 1939 expedition to the Petermann Ranges convinced once again of the need to establish a government base in the Range. The Docker River near Docker Gap was one of the three alternative sites he proposed. By 1939, he estimated there were only fifty to sixty people left living a traditional life in the Reserve; up to four hundred had moved to the margins of Alice Springs or Finke and to cattle stations along the southern edge of the MacDonnell Ranges. Strehlow and others were advocating that these people be drawn back from what Strehlow described as 'aimless wandering',

and re-established in the Petermann Ranges or the Haasts Bluff Reserve but the Chief Protector wrote, in a telling comment on Strehlow's earlier proposals: 'how much this can be effected, without depriving settlers of Aboriginal labour, is a matter of conjecture' (AA4). The creation of Ernabella Mission was taken as an excuse not to establish an administrative base in the central reserves and no action was taken by the government (AA5).

On the contrary, during 1939 the first moves were made to excise some portions of the Petermann Reserve and reopen them to White exploitation. E.W.P. Chinnery, the Director of Native Affairs, argued that the 'huge dimensions' of the reserve 'militate against effective control of the nomadic tribes' (AA6). C. Duguid considered that the impulse came rather from gold prospectors, who wanted access to the region, and he wrote of the proposed revision to the northern boundary that it was

> ...much too handy to the Petermann Ranges ... To create this corridor is to invite White men to drop into the Southern Reserve. (AA7)

As for requests to prospect for gold in the area, Duguid continued:

> I have received letters from people concerned with Lasseter's and other gold movements, all confirming my opinion that there is no gold there. These forays only serve to damage the natives.

According to Duguid, Chinnery had not visited the area himself and his argument was, therefore, presumably based on others' advice.

Strehlow, who also protested against the excision, pointed out that Ayers Rock would lie just one mile south of the proposed boundary. Since it possessed the only known permanent water in the area, parties travelling through the excised portion would need to visit Uluru (AA8). Despite these criticisms, the excision was made. In compensation, the Haasts Bluff Reserve was created further north (Long 1963, p.4.) Some of the lost country was later reincorporated in the Reserve, but other areas were not restored to Aboriginal ownership until the land claim of 1979.

Tourism

It was the desire to open the area to tourists that caused the loss of Uluru and Katatjuta from the surviving reserve. A campaign to gain access had been conducted throughout the 1950s. As early as 1951, for instance, Connellan Airways applied to the Director of Native Affairs for permission to build an airstrip at Uluru and to land there 'for an hour or so' with people who wanted to see and photograph the Rock. Even at that time, the Director expressed 'no great objection to the excision of Ayers Rock from the Reserve' (AA9). He opposed the idea of a tourist reserve not, apparently, from qualms about depriving the Aboriginal community of its sacred sites, but because there was no appropriate body to control tourist access (AA10).

A Native Affairs' patrol officer argued, however, that no natural waters should be surrendered from the Reserve or their availability prejudiced for the local people (AA11). Members of the public also objected. In 1953 the South Australian League of Women Voters wrote to the Northern Territory Administration:

> For the sake of white Australians, we feel that there is need for the strengthening of our moral code, and that we should not allow ourselves to break into this reserve; it is really the property of the Aborigines, and we strongly oppose any relaxing of the present regulations (AA12).

Similar sentiments were expressed by R. G. Hill in a letter to the Minister for Territories:

> Without being personal, your government and all past ones have a hideous record of injustice and greed that shocks any decent Australian whenever he thinks of the blackfellows. Can not the Ayers Rock area be left to reserve? ... To be quite honest I think that the government is not interested at all in the blackfellow but is doing a bit of trumpet blowing and window dressing and in private cursing them as a nuisance ... the whole affair, reeks to the high heavens with greed and injustice. (AA13).

Uluru and Katatjuta were nonetheless taken out of the reserve in 1958 (Commonwealth Gazette 20 December 1958). According to Bill Harney, (1969, pp.11 and 114), who became the first Ranger, the new tourist reserve was administered for its first year through the Native Welfare Branch, but the Northern Territory Reserves Board was created during 1958 to manage it as a tourist and wildlife reserve. When it was discovered that the Petermann Reserve had been improperly gazetted in 1920, the entire area was re-gazetted, but this time omitting Ayers Rock and the Olgas. Harney worked as Ranger until 1962, shortly before his death. The account in *To Ayers Rock and Beyond* describes Aboriginal visitors to the new Park during these five years, among them Nipper Winmati and Paddy Uluru (*see* Chapter 7).

After Harney's retirement, Aboriginal ties with Uluru were put under greater stress than ever. When F.G.G. Rose was at Angas Downs later in 1962, he found few Aboriginal people living at the Rock. He was blunt about the reason, writing:

> ... it is almost certain that if the Aborigines were not kept, or as it is expressed locally, 'hunted' away from the vicinity of Ayers Rock, the Aboriginal population at Angas Downs would largely transfer ... there (1965, p.57).

One of the most important sites was erroneously signposted 'the Kangaroo Tail' and tourists freely entered sites to which Aboriginal women and children had never been allowed access.

Hermannsburg Mission had established a ration depot at Haasts Bluff in 1940 and, in 1943, another at Areyonga. Although closer to Pitjantjatjara and Yankuntjatjara country, Areyonga was still well north of the Petermann Ranges and it lies in Western Aranda territory. Those who had stayed in the Reserve were encouraged to go to Areyonga in order to prevent them drifting closer to Alice Springs. This caused former neighbours among the Pitjantjatjara to find themselves separated by the 250 kilometres between Areyonga and Ernabella. J. Long reported that his questions in the early 1960s showed the majority of Areyonga people came from the Petermann Ranges and gave the name of places such as Piltati, Puta-puta, Kikingkura and Wangkari as their *ngura* (Long 1963, p.7); a 'handful' gave their country as Ayers Rock and Mount Olga. In 1953, responsibility for administering Areyonga was taken over by the government. Assimilation was the guiding policy, expressed by Areyonga's schoolteacher in a letter to the Senior Education Officer in 1953, where he describes settlement as a planned step in 'the breaking down of the tribal spirit' (AA14). This proved a difficult policy to implement because the people remained obstinately determined to preserve their own culture and hand it on to their children. How this was achieved is described in the next chapter.

CHAPTER 6

The Aboriginal response

In 1962 the anthropologist F.G.G. Rose made the rather narrowly Marxist prediction that Pitjantjatjara ritual would disappear following the destruction of the society's traditional subsistence economy. Admitting that ritual was in fact still flourishing twenty years after the pre-contact economy had been ruptured, he justified his prediction on the grounds that there must be a time lag while the Aboriginal people's consciousness adjusted to their new condition (1965, pp.84–5).

Some years later, Richard Gould criticised the Pitjantjatjara for having failed to transform their way of life and adapt to European contact. He saw them as dependent on White society and as losing their traditional culture without creating anything to take its place. In particular, they had failed to establish 'a viable relationship to the world market economy' (Gould & Fowler 1972, p.278). It could be pointed out that the Pitjantjatjara are not the only people having difficulties in this, but Gould is right to see that the Pitjantjatjara had to develop alternatives to the closed, subsistence economy that had supported them until the 1930s.

Notwithstanding the evidence that pastoralism had an overwhelming effect on the natural resources on which the subsistence economy was based, Aboriginal people moving in the area along the margin of pastoral settlement were still partly able to live off the bush. It is unlikely, however, that it could entirely support them. There is also evidence that, when bought flour was available, Aboriginal people preferred it to collecting and grinding bush seeds. (*see* Brokensha's account of preparing wild seeds, quoted in Chapter 2). Although they could no longer survive entirely by subsistence, people still travelled through the Uluru region, and despite the fact that Areyonga and Ernabella are 250 kilometres apart, people living in the two communities kept in contact.

The traveller A. Groom, at Areyonga in August 1947, while preparing to make an expedition to Uluru met sixty Pitjantjatjara men who had come from Ernabella to arrange an initiation ceremony with the Pitjantjatjara at Areyonga (1950, p.115). Later, as he returned from Uluru with Tiger Tjalkalyiri, Groom met other men travelling north toward Atila. As Groom's party moved eastward to the de Conlay's homestead, Tjalkalyiri exchanged smoke signals with this group as they walked from Witapula to Anari. He and his companions

> fired a great amount of spinifex, until we had a continuous screen of smoke behind us, defining our straightened course to all distant watchers; then towards evening the signals at Weetabilla [Witapula] commenced to creep out and extend one by one, up towards Mount Conner. The signaller was also now on the march. This strange converging of two lines of travel went on silently over the desert; it was weird, crystal clear, and filled with meaning. (1950, p.182)

Groom's description suggests that the group was following one of the traditional walking routes shown in Figure 1. He writes that some Ernabella people travelled to Hermannsburg or Areyonga for initiation ceremonies each year and comments that Aboriginal travellers now 'find their water fouled and shared by wandering stock, equipped and closed with man-made pumps and tanks' (p.178).

In 1951 an article appeared in *Holiday and Travel* recounting the expedition to Uluru a party of Sydney schoolboys made, accompanied by C.P. Mountford. The leader of the expedition describes how Mountford supervised the lighting of smoke signals and how answering smoke was seen from the Musgrave and Petermann Ranges. Eventually a party of Pitjantjatjara 'unable to speak English' arrived at Uluru. They brought three youths who were being initiated. The White schoolboys were allowed, through a certain amount of deception on Mountford's part, to watch some of the ceremony. At first the Aboriginal party argued that

> . . . our boys were of the same category as their own [and should be excluded] . . . but after much explanation by Mr Mountford, they were convinced our boys were initiated members of the 'white fella tribe'.

It is not possible to tell whether these Pitjantjatjara were people who still lived permanently in the bush or a group by then based at Ernabella or Areyonga.

During the early years of settlement life, the collection of dingo scalps was one of the main sources of income that allowed people to buy the stores they required to return to the bush. It was on 'dogging' trips that many people who are now young adults first saw their parents' estates. When he wrote his report recommending that Ernabella Station should be bought as a mission, J.R.B. Love argued against the new mission becoming a centre for trading dingo scalps, but church authorities decided that, on the contrary, it would buy scalps and pay the full bounty of seven shillings and sixpence on each one, less a small sum to cover 'administrative costs' (see AA15, AA16 and Melbourne *Herald* report of 28 May 1937). This rapidly drove independent White doggers out of business, and once they had left the district, Ernabella was able to acquire the abandoned leases (Hilliard 1968, pp.82 and 97). Dogging allowed Aboriginal people to produce goods (scalps) independently which they could exchange for clothes and food through the White economy, and it gave them a means of returning periodically to their own estates with children who had been born on the mission. For several years the mission encouraged people to do this by taking goods out to a pre-arranged point on the Reserve during the season when dingo pups are born and scalps most easily collected (Hilliard 1968, p.150). Family groups could also call at the mission periodically, exchange the scalps they had collected for rations, and then leave again for the bush. In 1953, a note was made by F.J.S. Wise,

the Administrator, that visits were being made to the Uluru area during the 'dogging' season between July and September of each year (AA17).

Gould & Fowler refer to 'dogging' in their paper but dismiss it as 'a small-scale activity' (1972, p.273). Small though it may have been in some terms, it was of central importance to Aboriginal culture during this critical period of transition. Bill Harney described Paddy Uluru and Nipper Winmati bringing their families to Uluru while on a dogging expedition. Minyintirri, a man whose estate lies near Docker River, was working with Harney and explained: 'Uluru and Winmarti with family and camel come up from my-country-way. All about been look-look for puppy dog.' Harney asked how the group had got its camel team and was told some had been caught and broken in by the party themselves, while others had been bought with dingo scalps from another Aboriginal (Harney 1969, p.135). Cassidy, one of Uluru's younger sons, told me he first saw the Rock during the time Harney was Ranger: 'What's that big sandhill?' he had asked his father as Uluru became visible above the horizon. 'That's my country,' his father replied. One of Cassidy's elder brothers, however, remembered camping with his father and family at Mutitjulu before tourists had begun to visit the Rock.

Areyonga was visited in August of 1961 by J.P.M. Long, then of the Welfare Branch's Research Section, who wrote that he came during the 'puppy season', when many people were out in the surrounding ranges in search of dingo scalps. Others, he continued, 'go south to the Alice Springs–Ayers Rock road and to Ayers Rock itself where they can trade artefacts with tourists' (Long 1963, p.5). Although the population of Areyonga was sometimes as high as 400, Long's check showed only 236 were actually there at the moment of his investigation. In April of 1964, Welfare Branch records show that the population of Areyonga dropped from about 700 to 261 in one month.

During the period which followed the creation of Ernabella and Areyonga, Aboriginal groups were able to increase greatly their mobility by adopting camels for transport. Camels were brought to the region by early explorers and settlers, and for the Pitjantjatjara to learn how to handle them took considerable adaptation. Gould & Fowler (1972) refer to feral camels being hunted for meat and criticise this as nothing more than an extension of traditional foraging methods. Remarkably, they neglect to record the success of the Pitjantjatjara in mastering the alien techniques of camel husbandry. Not only did they use these animals for their own purposes, but White travellers, such as the anthropologist C.P. Mountford (1950) and the writer A. Groom (1950), were also taken through the area by Aboriginal men with their own camel teams. Harney, describing Uluru and Winmati's arrival at the Rock, quotes Minyintirri's

account of how they had broken in camels they caught in the bush (1969, p.136). During the months of 1962 that F.G.G. Rose worked at Angas Downs, he saw Aboriginal people use camels to travel to Areyonga, Ayers Rock, the Petermann Ranges and Erldunda Station (Rose 1965, pp.22 and 28–9). W.E. Edwards told me that it was not until the major floods of 1974 that camels were finally replaced by motor transport, and Brokensha (1975, p.13) dates the availability of cars to about 1973. Certainly since the early 1970s, people of the region have made an equally remarkable adaptation to motor cars.

As tourism developed in central Australia during the 1960s, mobile parties of Aboriginal people became increasingly apparent to tourists and White authority. In 1964, an incident at Granite Downs, on the Stuart Highway across the South Australian border, brought this movement to the attention of the Welfare Branch's policy makers. An Aboriginal group was reported to have threatened some tourists in an attempt to sell them artefacts. One man tried to jump onto the moving car. As the driver accelerated he thought the man fell between car and caravan. A patrol officer went to investigate, but failed to discover any injured man, let alone a corpse. He did, however, find how widespread artefact sales had become.

During the 1960s, artefacts replaced dingo scalps as the principal source of independent income for Aboriginal groups. By the time of my fieldwork (1977–79), two classes of artefact were being manufactured for sale. One consisted of traditional implements, some (like spears) reduced to the size traditionally made as toys, the other class consisted of carved animal figures. All the animals and many artefacts were decorated with geometric patterns impressed with a heated piece of fencing wire. Although people sometimes carved animals that were among the dreamings of their estate, and although some burnt-wire designs incorporate motifs from the traditional art style, neither was part of the pre-contact culture, and their origin is obscure.

P. Brokensha, who has described the growth of European-organised craft production at Amata, since 1968 (1975, pp.68–9), is surely correct to identify the introduction of spinning and weaving by Ernabella Mission in the 1930s as one of the roots of contemporary artefact production. No doubt, too, Europeans have been obtaining traditional artefacts through various forms of exchange for as long as they have been in the area and so have introduced Aborigines to the idea of treating artefacts, like dingo scalps, as a saleable commodity.

According to F.G.G. Rose, burnt-wire decoration originated at Angas Downs in about 1960, at the suggestion of Arthur Liddle, the station owner, himself a man of Aboriginal descent (1965, p.93). Brokensha sees burnt-wire decoration as an extension of sand drawings, which are a traditional entertainment and art form (p.49). Rose believes it replaced the custom of incising decoration with the broken end of a length of wire. In his opinion, the carving of animal figures also originated at Angas Downs. He comments:

> What is remarkable is not that the old methods are lost but the virility that is shown in grappling with new problems under most unfavourable conditions. (p.96)

In the early 1960s, the road to Ayers Rock ran between Mount Ebenezer and Angas Downs homesteads. When Rose was at Angas Downs in 1962, he saw the manufacture of artefacts for sale to tourists, some of which he illustrated (1965, plates 23 and 26–9). Bill Harney has a perceptive eye-witness account of transactions between the people of Angas Downs and a coach party of tourists at the start of his book, *To Ayers Rock and Beyond* (1969, p.37). The tourists clearly believe that the correct behaviour is to haggle with the sellers until achieving the lowest possible price, a custom alien to Aboriginal culture. Rose estimated that in 1962, people selling artefacts were making about two pounds a week each (1965, p.68). By contrast, a four-week dogging trip yielded fourteen scalps (Rose 1965, p.71) providing a temporary income of five guineas a week. He noted that most artefacts were made by men and argued that this had reversed the pre-contact economic relationship between the sexes. Men no

Traditional
spear-thrower.

longer depended on their wives, the principal collectors of bush foods, but could now support them with purchased food from the station store (pp.78,80–1).

Rose considered that if it were not for their being 'hunted away' from Uluru, the Aboriginal community at Angas Downs would have moved to the Rock to trade with tourists there (p.57). However, many people were still avoiding a permanently settled life and, as with dingo scalping, it is doubtful whether they travelled solely to intercept tourists and make a profit from them.

Evidence for movement through the area during the 1960s is provided by Welfare Branch correspondence (summarised in Table 6). Consistent with government attitudes of the time, the Welfare Branch failed to recognise a strong attachment to Aboriginal culture in these groups; they saw simply a denial of conventional White values: the people were 'itinerant', 'loitering' or 'unemployed'. The Assistant Director wrote to tourist operators asking them to stop their customers paying Aborigines for artefacts or for taking photographs: 'the few shillings that the Aborigines make in this way tends to undo the work of my officers'. Giving money to people had 'an adverse effect in our attempt to teach the natives the principle of work for pay and make[s] them parasites on society'. The same letter contrasts the 'unsanitary' nature of roadside camps with the facilities for health care, education,

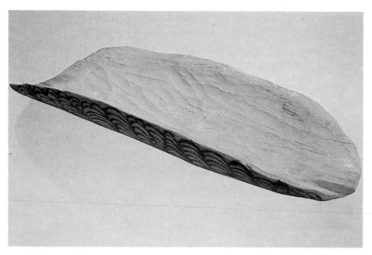

Traditional baby's cradle. Outside surface is decorated with burnt wire design incorporating *Kuniya* snake.

Carved and
decorated animal
figures (from rear:
perenti lizard,
brush-tail possum
and snake).

employment and training on settlements (WB1). The advantage of an education that helps Aboriginal people deal with our culture is undeniable, but these groups were not simply begging by the roadside; they were often engaged in educating their own children in the traditions of Aboriginal culture. The following year, one group was reported to be holding a ceremony at Mulga Park 'so that important tribal beliefs and rituals could be passed on from the elders to the up and coming influential middle-aged men'; the District Welfare Officer reported that 'it seems that their main object of being in the area is to carry out rituals that are important to them' (WB2).

Table 6 **Aboriginal presence in the Ayers Rock region during the mid-1960s**

Year	Date of report	Size and location of groups
1964	7 May	About 150–70 people camped at Wilpiya (Wilbia Well, on the old road to Ayers Rock via Angas Downs). Party includes 50 schoolchildren. Most had been there six weeks, some since December 1963.
	18 May	Wilbiya camp has declined to 80 people, only 20 of them from Areyonga. Most have returned to Areyonga, 10–12 to Ernabella, two small groups travelling between Erldunda and Mount Ebenezer.
	8 June	No one at Wilbiya; all returned to Angas Downs homestead or Areyonga.
	11 June	The 'Walkabout Group' seen at Mulga Park homestead, en route for Ernabella.
	24 August	No 'irregular' camps in the Ayers Rock area, but many former Areyonga residents thought to have moved to South Australia.
	9 October	96 temporary residents at Mulga Park for reburial ceremony. Mainly from Musgrave Park (Amata) and Ernabella. Include 25 in party led by Harry Brumby (Tjuwiri, a Kikingkura man), the 'last group not really settled' anywhere.
	21 December	20 Aboriginal people resident at Ayers Rock, 8 of them employed.
1965	16 February	Group seen at Victory Downs consisting of people from Amata, Mount Davies and Giles. Another group at Angas Downs; people who are always moving between Areyonga, Ernabella and intervening cattle stations.
	23 March	65 adults and 25 children from Areyonga at Wilpiya.

Year	Date of report	Size and location of groups
1965	n.d.	No Aboriginal people resident at Ayers Rock. Small party in Petermanns thought to have travelled there along route slightly north of Ayers Rock and the Olgas.
	10 June	15 people seen at Victory Downs, returning to Mount Cavenagh and De Rose Hill stations after holiday at Ernabella.
		Several groups participating in same ceremony, seen moving between Curtin Springs and Angas Downs: 25 people at Iyarrka, 17 people 17 miles east of Curtin Springs, 5 at Wilpiya; also smoke observed, indicating further parties travelling away from the road.
	28 October	Up to 250 had been present at Mulga Park for a ceremony; only 143 present on patrol officer's visit. Had come from Warburton, Mount Davies, Amata and Areyonga communities, Angas Downs, Mount Ebenezer, Victory Downs and Mulga Park stations.
1966	18 July	Half the labour force of Ernabella absent, most people moving toward Amata for initiation ceremonies.
		Captain No. 1 (Ikuta, a Kikingkura man) and 20 Areyonga residents between Mulga Park and Curtin Springs, collecting dingo scalps and looking for camels.
		Harry Brumby with a party of 30 near Curtin Springs, collecting dingo scalps.
		Another party near Curtin Springs waiting for Lively (Palingka, of Uluru) and 3 others to return from the Petermanns.
		58 people camped at Wilpiya, collecting dingo scalps and selling artefacts.
1967	30 August	Ceremony in progress at Mulga Park. Population has risen from 30 to 150 in five weeks.
	8th September	400 people have left Mulga Park, Ernabella and Amata to attend a ceremony in the Warburton Ranges.
1968	29 April	40 or more people, who in 1967 were living at Mulga Park, have moved to Curtin Springs. Living mainly off tourist revenue. Constitutes the 'principal walkabout group' led by Harry Brumby and Nipper Winmati.
		85 people living at Wilpiya.
	19 August	200 people from Angas Downs and Areyonga at Angas Downs for a ceremony.
	17 September	About 30 people led by Nipper Winmati camped at Iyarrka, selling artefacts. 12 others including Captain No. 1 and Tiger Tjalkalyiri waiting for Nipper's party at the Angas Downs turn-off.

expedient they were happy to forego when, as a patrol officer pointed out, the good rains had provided plenty of surface water and more game. The District Welfare Officer reported that in 1966 the seasonal movement of people out of Ernabella and Areyonga was the biggest for many years. Instead of just 'essential people', whole families had moved out to areas of ceremonial importance. He concluded:

> Although the important Aboriginal ceremonies were not discontinued during the drought years it is probable that they were curtailed to some extent ... because of the lack of 'bush tucker'. (WB5)

Two events seem to have brought this period to an end. The first was the founding of Docker River settlement. The chance to resettle permanently in the Petermann Ranges was provided in 1967 by the creation of this community on one of the sites proposed by T.G.H. Strehlow thirty years earlier. By 1968 the population of the new settlement was already three hundred, drawn from those whose country lay in the Petermanns and across to Uluru (personal communication from the Department of Aboriginal Affairs, Alice Springs). In that year the 'principal walkabout group', whose leaders were Nipper Winmati from Uluru and Tjuwirri Harry Brumby from Kikingkura, told a patrol officer they wanted to move to Docker taking their camels and an old truck. Another group, later in the year, said they would move to Docker when the ceremony they were conducting was over. Susan

Woenne has described the return to Docker (1977).

The second event was a radical shift in government policy during the early 1970s, a summary of which can be found in Mr Justice Toohey's report on the Warlpiri land claim (1979a). It was realised that the policy of collecting people together in settlements and missions had to a large extent failed. Various Aboriginal groups approached the Department of Aboriginal Affairs (the federal body that took over from the Welfare Branch), saying that they wanted to leave settlements and move back to their own country, partly to maintain their traditional links with the land and partly to escape the pressures of life among groups with whom they would not traditionally have lived. The development of the outstation movement among Pitjantjatjara people in South Australia is described by Peter Brokensha (1975, pp.13–15; for the outstation movement in Kakadu see Fox 1977, pp.42–3). A number of outstations developed around Docker River and two, including that at Cave Hill (Wallace & Wallace 1977), in the Musgrave Ranges.

During 1977–79, the Aboriginal community at Uluru closely resembled these outstations in size and composition. Although the Ayers Rock community lacked the autonomy that comes from living on land to which White access is controlled and Aboriginal title recognised, circumstances had improved since the 1960s.

Despite predictions that Pitjantjatjara and Yankuntjatjara religion would collapse, and despite attempts to destroy it, the religion has survived. In July of 1953, the schoolteacher at Areyonga, in the letter that referred to a planned step in breaking down the tribal spirit, complained that Pitjantjatjara children showed more interest in attending traditional ceremonies than his classes:

> During the following weekend, a large proportion of the natives here left on a walkabout to Jay Creek for corroborees and initiation purposes . . . Although I have gained the confidence of the old men and others of the tribe to some extent, I was not able to persuade them to leave their children at school here while they were away . . . Many children seemed to be more interested in the treatment they were receiving than they ever had been in school work. (AA18)

Their religion is still of utmost importance to the Yankuntjatjara and Pitjantjatjara today. The fact that authority to speak on religious matters belongs to the older men creates a misleading impression that the younger are unknowledgeable or uninterested in legend and ritual. As I grew to know people better, I became impressed with the depth of concern that many young adults feel for the perpetuation of their ancestral traditions, a concern they expressed in private or when authorised to do so by older men. It is true that economic change has had some effect, although not to the degree predicted by F.G.G. Rose. N. Wallace (1977) has published a detailed discussion of the relation between economy and religion at Amata and Ernabella, in which he describes how the specific constraints of wage-earning modified the sequence of ceremonial life without destroying it.

Since the 1930s, Aboriginal culture has undergone a transformation brought about by contact with White society. Change has taken place in technology, productive activities and settlement pattern. First camels then motors have replaced long-distance travel on foot. Steel axes and knives have replaced those of stone. A substantial part of the diet consists of purchased food made available by the national economic and trading system. Settlement is more permanent, a development made possible by supplying water from bores and importing food supplies. What has not changed is a knowledge of the topography of the bush: names for places, the traditional *inma* song cycles, the location of water, the division of the land into 'countries' or estates. This knowledge today provides the means of validating residence, and political and ceremonial roles in Aboriginal law. It is also a crucial requirement for a successful land claim.

Why has the religion survived despite the predictions of Rose and government officials? Even from Rose's perspective, one reason is apparent: people have not entirely given up their reliance on bush foods, nor have they completely entered the market economy. But it should be clear from the discussion in Chapter 1 that Pitjantjatjara and Yankuntjatjara religion is something more than a reflection of traditional economic roles: it provides a comprehensive image of the people's place in their world, both as individuals and as groups. Throughout their history of contact with European society, the Pitjantjatjara and Yankuntjatjara have never been given any reason to see themselves as an integral part of the dominant society. On the contrary they have constantly been reminded that, in the minds and deeds of others, they still occupy a unique economic and cultural position in central Australia. Not only is this an important reason for the persistence of their religion, but their possession of this distinctive world view has also played a crucial part in helping them to see themselves not, as Richard Gould would have had it, as failed dependants on White Australian society, but as representatives of a positive, alternative way of life.

PART THREE

Land rights

Figure 5
Location of Uluru,
Kakadu National
Parks and
Pitjantjatjara lands

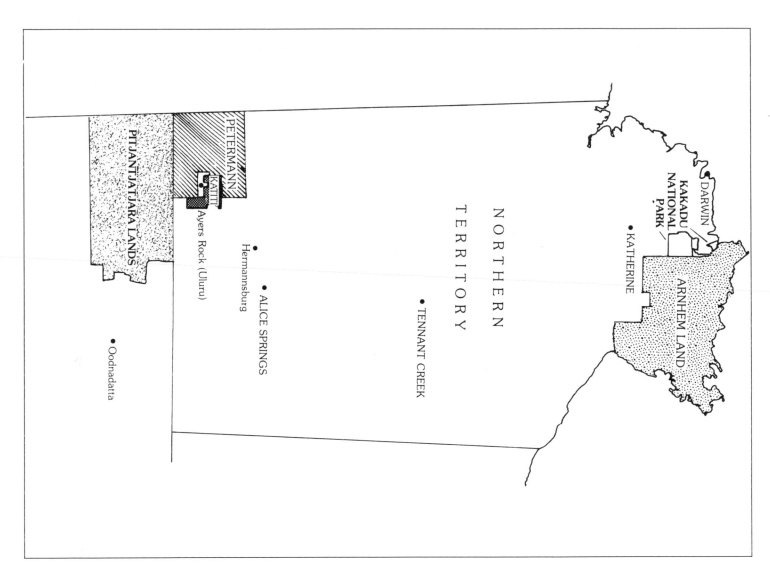

CHAPTER 7

The recognition of Aboriginal rights

The survival of Aboriginal owners of Uluru was discovered by government agencies in November 1971, when members of the federal Office of Aboriginal Affairs and the South Australian Department of Community Welfare attended a meeting at Ernabella to discuss policies and programs for Aboriginal development in the Pitjantjatjara area of north-west South Australia. An Office of Aboriginal Affairs official suggested that Pitjantjatjara people apply for one of the business leases then being opened at Ayers Rock. Aboriginal men held a separate discussion during the course of this meeting, at which Paddy Uluru and others spoke passionately of the sacred places at Uluru and their desecration by tourists. What the men said was transcribed by Andy Tjilari and translated by the Reverend Bill Edwards; passages have since been quoted by the Wallaces in their book *Killing me Softly* (1977, p.60) and in Jenny Isaacs' *Australian Dreaming* (1980, pp.40–1).

Paddy Uluru spoke of the Rock as his place, appealing to the government in Canberra to help him protect the places with which his fathers and grandfathers had entrusted him. Tony Tjamiwa, whose country is linked to Uluru by the Mala Wallaby dreaming track, supported him, emphasising the ceremonial importance of Uluru. Other senior men asked the federal Government to help protect the sites. Although these communities were by now well-used to selling artefacts and carvings to Europeans, no one spoke

93

of wanting to make money from the Rock's dreaming places or stories; it was their exploitation in this way by White people that concerned them. (A store selling artefacts and general goods to tourists was later set up in the Park by the Docker River community.)

About four months later, Uluru and twenty-five other senior men went to the Rock and held an *inma* ceremony there. They pointed out some of the most sacred places to the Head Ranger, asking him to help prevent tourists from entering places forbidden to the uninitiated, and to remove some of the notices that wrongly identified dreaming places.

In the following July (1973) the federal House of Representatives Standing Committee on Environment and Conservation visited the area while preparing a report on the Ayers Rock–Mount Olga National Park. After meeting White tourist operators and conservation experts, members of the Committee went to Mimili, Ernabella and Docker River to talk to Aboriginal people associated with Ayers Rock. A meeting which the Committee members considered most significant was held with Paddy Uluru and others at Mimili. Paddy Uluru gave them the impression he feared and mistrusted White people at the Rock, largely because of 'the circumstances of his removal from the area and the alleged killing of his brother by Whites on the same occasion' (Standing Committee on Environment and

Conservation Report 1973, p.11). He told the Committee about the great importance of Uluru in traditional life and said that he and a number of others wanted to go back to live there. He was anxious to explain and hand on the stories to his son (Paddy Uluru had in fact five sons) before he died and to have access to some parts of the Rock completely closed. Perceptively, the Committee appreciated the difficulty men like Uluru had in speaking freely to White people, when they had known them almost always as invaders and bosses, suggesting that every possible encouragement should be given to them to state their views on how the Park should be managed, even though circumstances tended 'to make them diffident in expressing even the most strongly held opinions' (1973, p.13). In its report, the Committee pointed out that the area gained a special character from its traditional Aboriginal associations. 'In the future,' it concluded, 'the traditional rights of Aboriginals must be assured and ... a central role in responsibility for management will rest with them' (p.13).

When the Committee prepared its report, the Woodward Commission on Aboriginal Land Rights had only recently begun its investigation. Implicitly acknowledging that the Park could be claimed by its traditional owners, the report argued that, because Ayers Rock had already become a symbol of the outback for all Australians, plans to protect the Rock and surrounding country from over-use should be put into effect immediately, rather than wait for Mr Justice Woodward's conclusions (H.A. Jenkins et al. 1973, pp.4–5). It recommended that the soon-to-be-established federal Parks and Wildlife Service should be given overall control of the Park but suggested nine ways in which Aboriginal people could be involved in the Park's management. Many of these suggestions were carried out: an Aboriginal camp site was established on the south side of the Rock, with its own bore (Bore 29); the most important sites were protected by a fence; an Advisory Committee with Aboriginal members was established, and Aboriginal rangers were appointed.

It could be argued that, like the Ranger Commission in the Kakadu area, the Committee should have waited for publication of the Woodward reports. But Justice Woodward's inquiries were at a much earlier stage, and the area was already well-established as a Park. Eventually Justice Woodward recommended that because of its importance to tourism, Ayers Rock should be treated as a special case, a recommendation that could well have been carried out by reaching an agreement with the traditional owners, similar to that later reached at Kakadu. Unfortunately this was not yet to be the case.

The Ayers Rock Advisory Committee first met in March 1974. By December of that year it had established, with the help of the Reverend Jim Downing and Jim Lester of the Institute of Aboriginal Development in Alice Springs, a list of senior men linked directly or indirectly with Uluru and Katatjuta. They included Paddy Uluru and his sons, Nipper Winmati and his brother Lively Palingka, Bill and Nelson Ukai (younger cousins of Winmati and Palingka); Peter Bulla and his brother Tjalkalyiri Tiger, whose father came from the Petermann Ranges, but who grew up around Uluru and Katatjuta; Toby Nangina and Nyinnga Stewart of Atila; Pompy Douglas, whose mother's father came from Uluru, and Tony Tjamiwa, custodian of the Mala dreaming across the South Australian border.

During 1976, when the House of Representatives Standing Committee again investigated Ayers Rock, it was told by Mr Huey of the Department of Aboriginal Affairs that the Advisory Committee's meetings had all been attended by at least half a dozen Aboriginal people. Paddy Uluru had been present at a number, and there had sometimes been more Aboriginal than White people (*Hansard* report of Committee hearings, December 1976, p.108, *see also* p.26). Unfortunately, by 1976 Paddy Uluru and other men were becoming tired of repeated meetings that had no apparent results. In Pitjantjatjara custom, one does not constantly consult people on particular issues, since they expect only to give their answer once.

The appointment of three Aboriginal Rangers

had also led to difficulties, largely owing to the un-Aboriginal work patterns expected of them. All but one found it difficult to act as guides to tourists. They were unhappy talking about the legends, and some found it hard to adjust to regular working hours every day. Toby Nangina was successful as a guide to the animals and plants in the Park, but other members of the Aboriginal community resented that a few should be earning wages from the Rock when they were not. It was this resentment which led, I believe, to the most successful Aboriginal Ranger resigning, and leaving the community for several months. Mr Huey appreciated the problems that the job entailed, 'It is a pretty difficult role to ask an Aborigine to play. He is virtually asked to be a public relations man to international and local tourists.' Huey also understood the feelings of Aboriginal rangers who were confined to cleaning toilets and emptying rubbish bins (*Hansard*, 2 December 1976, p.107).

Paradoxically the one senior man who showed an interest in charging money to see sacred aspects of the Rock was criticised for his mercenary approach by the very Whites who otherwise despaired of the difficulty Aboriginal people had in adopting White roles. His plan did not materialise, and it is very doubtful that the Aboriginal community would have allowed him to go ahead with it.

Nonetheless, Aboriginal involvement in the Park had increased dramatically since the time during the 1960s when they were 'hunted away'. Paddy Uluru did not return to live at the Rock immediately the bore and camping area were established, but he had settled there before the start of my fieldwork in September 1977 and remained until his death in 1979, when he was buried near his camp at Bore 29. During those two years he took several of his sons on visits to important places around the Rock. After Paddy's death, Toby Nangina, who was also living at the camp at Bore 29, took over his role as teacher. Palingka, C.P. Mountford's and T.G.H. Strehlow's instructor, also returned to live at the Rock until he died. Because they were living near Uluru and Katatjuta, these and other senior men who survived them were able to visit sacred sites, ensure that they had not been damaged, and perform the appropriate rituals. People were also able, in their own time, to carve animals for sale to tourists. Although vulnerable to the haggling that Harney described at Angas Downs, this provided them with a little extra money. Paddy Uluru made many expeditions into the bush to collect mulga for boomerangs, or spear bush for spears. One one occasion at Katatjuta, he had exchanged some lengths of spear wood for cigarettes within minutes, as a coach party toiled up Walpa Pulka, the 'Valley of the Wind', and passed him walking down. There have been times, too, when the public songs of the Kuniya *inma*, which tell how parties of Carpet Snake ancestors crossed the sandhill country to the east and met up at Uluru, have been sung to tourists. Derek Roff, the Head Ranger, is probably correct to suggest, as he has done, that one of the best things about the return of Aboriginal people to the Rock is the opportunity it gives White people to meet and talk to these people in their own country.

On the negative side, there is no doubt that Aboriginal people still felt frustrations imposed by the Park regime. They could not move camp as they wished but were confined to Bore 29, or a camp near the store and caravan park, which some had established on their own initiative. Those in the closer camp were vulnerable to tourists, who invaded their privacy, sometimes taking photographs without permission. In 1977–79 their housing was still well below the standard appropriate to settled camps. There were restrictions on hunting and collecting firewood within the Park. Alcohol could not be excluded from the camps because, despite the wish of many senior Aboriginal people to control it, they did not have the right to enforce their own regulations. Neither the Territory Reserves Board nor the Australian National Parks Service contemplated an equal partnership with the traditional owners, and the Aboriginal community was repeatedly forced to seek piecemeal concessions from the Park authorities.

By 1976, Ayers Rock had become a major asset to the Northern Territory economy. Witnesses to the House of Representatives Standing Committee's 1976 Inquiry considered that about half the people who visited Alice Springs also went to the Rock, which suggested the Rock was one of the Centre's main tourist attractions. One witness estimated Uluru was worth between $5 million and $15 million a year in tourist revenue. Senator Kilgariff gave evidence that tourism had overtaken the pastoral industry as the Centre's main source of income and that Alice Springs, although it began as a supply centre for pastoralists, now depended to a far greater extent on tourism. A witness from the federal Department of Industry and Commerce suggested that Uluru was second only to the Great Barrier Reef as 'some way in which we can sell Australia as a destination for overseas visitors' (*Hansard*, 2 December 1976, p.82).

Although the Australian National Parks and Wildlife Service had taken over supervision of the Park following the Standing Committee's 1973 Report, in 1976 the Northern Territory Self-Government Act was in preparation, which would give the Territory's government control of all Crown Land within its borders except that specifically reserved for the Commonwealth. The decision to reserve the National Park for the National Parks and Wildlife Service was taken at a meeting in October 1976 between Professor Ovington, Director of the Service, Mr Letts,

Majority Leader in the Northern Territory Legislative Assembly, and representatives of the Department of the Northern Territory and the Northern Territory Reserves Board.

One recommendation made by the Standing Committee in 1973 but not carried out was to extend the Park northwards, taking in an area of low rocky hills and the surrounding sand dunes called Yulara, or the 'Sedimentaries'. This had been advised on ecological grounds, because the Park is relatively small and vulnerable to the disturbances inevitably caused by the large number of visitors. The recommendation was not adopted, because Yulara was vacant Crown Land and the Department of the Northern Territory included it in the areas 'frozen' pending Aboriginal land claims.

While the Standing Committee was carrying out its 1976 inquiries, a visit to Yulara was organised by the Central Land Council and Department of Aboriginal Affairs, to obtain information about its significance from those Aboriginal people associated with the area. Four reports were prepared on this visit, one each by the Central Land Council and Department of Aboriginal Affairs representatives, and two by the Areyonga schoolteacher and Amata minister knowledgeable about Pitjantjatjara culture, who had both acted as interpreters.

Most of the senior men were present, including Pompy Douglas, Tjalkalyiri Tiger, Napala Jack, Nipper Winmati, Toby Nangina and Paddy Uluru's son Cassidy Uluru. Paddy himself was missing, having said that he was 'sick of meetings', a sentiment echoed by those men who did attend. In one of the interpreter's words,

> Considerable emphasis was placed on the tedious nature of the discussions held from time to time without much apparent progress … The older people in particular feel they have said all that needs to be said: they do not wish to go over the same ground again.

On 23 November the party drove through the Sedimentaries, along part of an old road to Giles Meterological Station, visiting one of the two dreaming sites in the area and pointing out the route of an important dreaming track running from Katatjuta to Lake Amadeus.

Asked about the way in which Aboriginal people held responsibility for looking after dreaming places, the men spoke of how dreaming tracks gave rise to shared responsibility among many groups (see Chapter 3). They also said they did not want Yulara to be separated in any way from Uluru or Katatjuta. They did not wish to stop tourism, and they were happy to see the National Park continue to operate, provided their various requests for improved conditions were met. Among these, they said, were better protection for sacred places, better housing for residents and visitors, and permission to camp where they wished within the Park (it had been suggested that

Aboriginal people should be removed, with White visitors, to the proposed tourist village). Some also wanted to build two 'museums' near the Rock, which could be used partly to lock up sacred objects and partly as work centres for making artefacts.

There is no evidence to suggest that the men saw any conflict between the existence of a National Park and their own traditional rights to the area. One interpreter reported that they had great difficulty even understanding the different jobs of the Land Council and Park authorities. When I first discussed the procedures involved in making a claim with some of the senior men the following year, their reaction was one of incredulity that it should be necessary to prove to the Government the traditional title they held. This was understandable, considering that for about five years the Federal and Territory Governments had regularly consulted them as if they were the area's Aboriginal owners.

On 10 January 1977, about three months after the decision had been taken to declare the Park under the Commonwealth National Parks and Wildlife Conservation Act, the Director of the Australian National Parks Service, Professor Ovington, visited Uluru to talk with Aboriginal people about the decision. The meeting was poorly attended; only four of the senior traditional owners of the Rock were there, together with six men from countries in the Petermann Ranges. Central Land Council and Department of Aboriginal Affairs reports describe what took place. Those present were invited to make suggestions for incorporation into the National Parks Service's plan of management, although Ovington explained that until the Park had been declared under federal legislation, no such plan could be drawn up and he was unable to make promises. Represented through a younger relative, the men spoke about how hunting restrictions in the Park concerned them. The desire for 'museums' and better housing was again mentioned. Most importantly, the men put forward a proposal to move the National Park's boundaries northward, so as to exclude Uluru, Katatjuta and Yulara. These would become Aboriginal land. Tourists would still have free access to the area, but all Aboriginal rights would be maintained and sacred sites protected. Ovington told them that the park boundaries would remain where they were, to which the men reeplied that they would not then agree to Yulara becoming part of the Park. Although unhappy about agreeing to federal administration of the Park when Ovington was unable to guarantee that he could include their requests in the Plan of Management, they appeared to consider that federal administration would be preferable to control by the Northern Territory Government. The Land Council's representative concluded his report:

The general consensus ... was that if and only if the above conditions (access for hunting, better housing, etc.) were met the National Parks and Wildlife Services' intention to have the Park declared under Federal Legislation should be adopted.

After this meeting, it occurred to both the Central Land Council and the Department of Aboriginal Affairs in Alice Springs that an Aboriginal Land Claim on the Park might be excluded by the federal National Parks legislation. Mr Huey raised this at the next meeting of the Advisory Committee, at which Paddy and Cassidy Uluru and Toby Nangina were present, but he was later told by his central office in Canberra that the National Park could still be claimed because the Crown still held it. The Department of Aboriginal Affairs also telegraphed their head office to report that since many key figures (including Uluru and his sons, Winmati, Nyinnga Stewart, Toby Nangina and Tony Tjamiwa) were not present, the meeting with Ovington on 10 January would have to be considered something of a disaster.

The statement that the Park could still be claimed proved to be true only until 24 May that year, when the declaration of the Park under the Commonwealth National Parks and Wildlife Conservation Act came into effect. For a number of reasons the Central Land Council did not formally lodge a claim on vacant Crown Land including Yulara until 1 December 1978, and revised this claim to include the National Park only on 19 February 1979. Doubt as to the legal status of the Land Council when the Land Rights Act was first passed, confusion as to the status of the National Park under the Act and the wish not to compromise negotiations with the Commonwealth National Parks Service inhibited the Council from taking action earlier.

The Land Rights Act in the Northern Territory

Government support for the outstation movement was an important step toward giving Aboriginal people more control over their own affairs, but the Northern Territory Land Rights Act was far more influential in reversing the assimilation policy. Reserves had once been seen as temporary sanctuaries where Aboriginal people could live until 'the time is ripe for [their] further development' (see Chapter 5), but the Land Rights Act gave title to reserves to the Aboriginal owners and provided a limited opportunity for them to claim other land. The Act accepted the importance of traditional ties to the land in Aboriginal society, and it conceded that tradition was a continuing force in Aboriginal society. The Act, as passed in 1976, was the outcome of several years' inquiry by the Woodward Commission and, despite modification by the Fraser Government, which was then in power, largely fulfilled its original intention. In 1979, the legislation was put to work when the Central Land Council presented its third land claim, a claim to the Ayers Rock National Park and surrounding country.

The Act deals with the administration of Aboriginal land, including all the Aboriginal Reserves that existed in the Territory at the time the Act was introduced. It defines how land councils are to be constituted and managed, under what conditions mining companies can operate on Aboriginal land, and how mining royalties should be administered. One important section makes it possible for Aboriginal groups to claim those parts of their traditional territory that lie on vacant Crown Land; that is, land that belongs to the Crown, over which no one holds a pastoral, commercial or mining lease, and which is not included in a town boundary or set aside for a public purpose. The Act also allows Aboriginal people to claim land leased to them by the Crown.

In order to stop a claim being pre-empted by the alienation of the land, the federal and Northern Territory governments agreed to a temporary 'freeze' on all vacant Crown Land over which claims had been lodged, or notice of which had been given, and not to alienate any of this land until the relevant claims had been determined.

The Act is scrupulously careful in defining which Aboriginal people may claim any piece of unalienated land; it is only those who are found to be its 'traditional Aboriginal owners'. Section 3 of the Act sets out to define the essential features of land ownership according to Aboriginal tradition throughout the Northern Territory.

Section 50 of the Act defines how to make a land claim. Each claim is heard before an Aboriginal Land Commissioner. The Commissioner must decide whether the Aboriginal claimants match up to the Act's definition of traditional ownership, and whether the land they claim is unalienated. He must also measure the strength of their traditional attachment to the land claimed and their desire to live on it. He then recommends to the federal Minister for Aboriginal Affairs whether or not title to the land should be given to a land trust made up of the traditional owners and those other Aboriginal people traditionally allowed to use and occupy the land. At the same time, he must comment on the number of Aboriginal people who would be advantaged by a successful claim (these may be many more than the traditional owners), the nature and extent of their advantage, the detriment that any other people may suffer from a successful claim, and the effect of a successful claim on land use in the area. Mining companies, commercial fishermen and neighbouring pastoralists have frequently appeared in claim hearings, arguing that the disadvantage they will suffer from all or part of the claim being successful would outweigh the benefit to the Aboriginal claimants, either because of more difficult access

Reserve. The Ranger Inquiry was set up to investigate the potential effects on the environment of proposed uranium mining in the Ranger area. Its hearings began in September 1975. By the time the Inquiry's first report was delivered in October 1976, the Commission appreciated that the Land Rights Act was likely to be relevant to its investigation and the Act, when formulated, contained a special section allowing the Ranger Inquiry to determine whether or not there was a group, or groups, of Aborigines entitled to use and occupy vacant Crown Land within the region.

The Ranger Inquiry found that there were clans owning estates in the region, although some of their land lay in the Reserve (and would, therefore, become theirs when the Act was passed) and some on pastoral leases, which could, therefore, not be claimed. Thirteen clans were found to hold estates which were all, or partly, on vacant Crown Land.

The Director of the Australian National Parks and Wildlife Service had announced his intention to recommend the creation of a National Park (Kakadu) in the region, but the land intended for the Park was largely still unalienated at the time of the Ranger Inquiry. When it was found that there were traditional Aboriginal owners of the land, title was given to them by the Federal Government, and the Kakadu National Park was established by leasing the land from the traditional owners.

The Park's Plan of Management gave considerable recognition to Aboriginal interests, based primarily on conditions included in the Park's Lease Agreement. The Plan aims to maintain 'Park values' for the Aboriginal people and give special protection to Aboriginal art sites, sacred sites and other sites of significance; to establish a management program in which Aboriginal people traditionally associated with the Park play a major role; to assist traditional owners to settle in the Park; and to involve interested groups in developing and carrying out Park management (see Ovington 1980, section 25.5).

Several outstations were set up within the Park and a number of the traditional owners have become Park Rangers. Although some Aboriginal Rangers have been reluctant to direct White tourists, they play an important role in regulating hunting and gathering, in visiting painting sites to guard against vandalism, and in research into the Park's plant and animal resources. There is no doubt that their recognition as traditional owners and their involvement in Park management have enormously raised Aboriginal morale. It is a far cry from the days when they worked as unpaid labourers for itinerant buffalo shooters, or were prevented by station managers from camping and hunting on their land.

CHAPTER 8

The Uluru land claim

The land claim and the National Park

A successful land claim on Uluru would have given the Aboriginal community a chance to negotiate a role in the management of the Park, like that achieved by the traditional owners at Kakadu. But their claim was heavily opposed. When hearings opened in Alice Springs on 2 April 1979, lawyers representing both the Territory Government and the Commonwealth argued that the Park was not eligible to be claimed.

Many of the Aboriginal claimants had travelled into Alice for the hearing and there was considerable interest in the national press. The Land Commissioner agreed first to hear legal argument on the admissability of a claim over the Park, and after two days hearing, retired to consider his judgment, which he delivered on 4 April. The Commissioner found that, when the Park had been declared under the Commonwealth National Parks Act on 24 May 1977, this alienated title from the Crown and gave it to the Director of the Australian National Parks Service (Toohey 1980, pp.34–5). It could not, therefore, now be claimed under the Land Rights Act. Satisfactory though this may have been to the governments, and to motel owners and tour operators who supposed a claim might damage tourist development, the Commissioner's decision was a devastating shock to the Aboriginal owners, many of whom had only recently come to terms with the

105

need to prove their traditional title to the Government.

Immediately the Commissioner had announced his finding that the Park was alienated land, senior claimants together with the Central Land Council's chairman, Wenten Rabuntja, spoke to reporters outside the hall:

> That's my place out there, said Nipper Winmati, the White fella knows no stories out there. That's my place, I own, my father was born there and I was born there. White fellas haven't got their stories or dreamings out there—I don't try and take away Melbourne or Adelaide ... we want the White men to come and visit our place, not take it away. They must know it belongs to us. Now I am left with just my tent and broken promises.

Bill Ukai commented that White men wanted Uluru for making money, but Aboriginal men also wanted it for they were its owners and keepers of its sacred places (reported in Adelaide *Advertiser*, 5 April 1979 and Melbourne *Age* 7 April 1979).

Wenten Rabuntja pointed out that the National Park had been declared after the enactment of the Land Rights Act, during the period which the Commonwealth and Territory Governments had agreed to a freeze on any moves to change the status of unalienated Crown Land and, more specifically, while the Director of the Australian National Parks and Wildlife Service was negotiating with traditional owners of land in the Park. 'The C.L.C. [Central Land Council] does not criticise his Honour for making this decision on the law', said Wenten, 'the law he had to interpret had been deliberately altered by the Federal Government to make this decision inevitable' (reported in *The Sydney Morning Herald*, Adelaide *Advertiser*, *Northern Territory News*, and *Canberra Times*, 5 April 1979).

The same day, a press release was issued by the Pitjantjatjara Council in Amata condemning the alienation of the Park and pointing out that many Pitjantjatjara people in the region had links with Uluru through ceremonies and dreaming stories. The statement went on to call on the Federal Government to offer the Aboriginal claimants a freehold title with a lease back to the Australian National Parks Service and a joint management program. It pointed out that just such an agreement was already operating in the Kakadu National Park and commented, 'A failure to offer such a solution makes incredible any claim by the Commonwealth that they support meaningful Land Rights for Aboriginal people'.

By coincidence, the National Aboriginal Congress was meeting at the same time in Canberra. *The Canberra Times* reported that, 'the N.A.C. [National Aboriginal Congress] representative from the area, Mr Billy Stockman, wept when he heard that the claim had been disallowed. At lunch time he sat alone and dejected in a courtyard at Parliament House.' Mr Stockman moved a resolution at the meeting which read: 'That the Pitjantjatjara and

Yankuntjatjara people have the spiritual significance of these two areas [Uluru and Katatjuta] and that this link is with *every* Aboriginal tribe throughout Australia. But the legal rights remain with Pitjantjatjara and Yankuntjatjara people' (*The Canberra Times*, 5 April 1979).

The same day, the Minister for Aboriginal Affairs issued a statement pointing out that the freeze applied only to land over which claims had already been announced and that the Central Land Council had not lodged a claim on the Park until two years after the Commonwealth had first declared its intention of proclaiming the Park under Commonwealth legislation. At a meeting in January 1977, he said the traditional owners had indicated that they only wanted to claim areas surrounding the Park, including the Sedimentaries, which had, therefore, been omitted from the land handed to the National Parks Service. This was not the Land Council's recollection. As Wenten Rabuntja reported, they believed the traditional owners had merely agreed to defer a claim until the National Parks Service had shown it could improve living conditions and Aboriginal involvement in Park management (news sources cited above). This view was supported by the National Aboriginal Congress which, answering the Minister's statement, said that the meeting he referred to had ended on the understanding that further discussions would be held with the National Parks Service before any action was

taken (*The Canberra Times*, 5 April 1979). The Minister's statement that traditional owners only wanted to claim the Sedimentaries differs from the reports of those who attended the meeting on 10 January 1977, and in implying a general acceptance it overlooks the fact that many crucial owners were missing from the meeting with Professor Ovington.

Two days after the Commissioner's finding, the traditional owners drew up a petition to present to the Prime Minister, in which they also made the proposal put forward by the Pitjantjatjara Council. It read:

> We the undersigned are the traditional owners of Uluru and Katatjuta and have taken these from our ancestors as of right since the Dreamtime.
> The Whiteman has known of these places for only a little time and he cannot own them and they are not his country.
> We accept that our land is of interest to people all over Australia and from overseas and we are happy for them to visit and see our place. We agree to our land including a National Park.
> We cannot accept however, that someone else in Canberra can hold the papers to our land. It is not his country — it is ours. White people should show their recognition of our rights and give us the freehold title. We will make an agreement to lease the land to the National Parks Service if we can have a say about what is done. We must protect our law, our sacred places from visitors. These are for Aboriginals alone and essential to us if our culture is to survive.

We ask you, the Prime Minister, to help us with what we ask. We are not greedy. We only wish to keep the land of our fathers for ourselves and our children.

Mr Fraser was in Alice Springs that day so, accompanied by Ross Howie, the Land Council's lawyer, they attempted to meet him at his motel. After waiting two hours, they were allowed to hand over the petition, but not to talk. As the Adelaide *Advertiser* reported, 'Mr Fraser said: "I can't speak with you, I have to go and do the job I came here for." [He] ... then left for the main street where about 300 townspeople were waiting for him to lay the foundation stone to Alice Springs' new Civic Centre ' (*see also Hobart Mercury* and *The Canberra Times*, 7 April 1979).

Winmati and Peter Bulla flew to Melbourne with the Land Council's lawyer and attempted, again unsuccessfully, to see Mr Fraser on 10 April. Both men insisted their claim would not affect tourism: 'We will welcome visitors to our area' said Mr Winmati, and Peter Bulla also told reporters that tourists were welcome (Melbourne *Age* and Melbourne *Sun*, 11 April 1979).

That day and the next, two of Australia's leading papers carried editorials arguing that title to Uluru and Katatjuta should be granted to their traditional owners. On 10 April *The Australian* wrote that a successful claim would deprive no one of access, no mining developments would be prevented, nor would an increase in tourist activity. The claimants had promised to lease the area on the same basis as the Kakadu National Park, and by giving them title, 'the Government will keep faith with the many Aborigines who regard the Uluru land claim as the most significant they have ever made'. The Melbourne *Age* wrote the following day that the Federal Government seemed to have acted at the very least with stealth to prevent traditional Aboriginal ownership of the Ayers Rock–Olgas area being established. The writer in the *Age* saw land claims as limited by law, based on natural justice, undoing a little of the havoc of the past and holding out some hope for a better future.

That day, a successful meeting with the Prime Minister finally took place. This meeting was widely reported (*see The Australian* and *Northern Territory News* for 12 April 1979, *The Canberra Times* and *Centralian Advocate* for 14 April 1979). Mr Fraser was reported to have said he well understood the deep attachment the traditional owners had with their land. According to *The Australian*, 'government sources' stated that the National Park would be temporarily rescinded to allow the granting of the Aboriginal claim and the leasing back of the land. 'Blacks Win Rock Back' said the headline in the *Northern Territory News*.

During the meeting Mr Everingham, the Northern Territory's Chief Minister, intervened by phone to say that he had a proposal that might suit all parties, and it was agreed that these proposals would be put to the traditional owners and the Central Land Council before the federal

Government took any further action. Senator Chaney, the Minister for Aboriginal Affairs, said he would keep the matter in front of the Federal Government. Peter Bulla and Winmati released a statement in which they again emphasised that they did not want to stop tourists coming to Ayers Rock, and they spoke of the Rock's significance:

> We have the knowledge of these stories and places.
> The Aboriginal law connected with those stories and places is still strong ... The ceremonies are still happening. Young people are learning the stories and the law from the old people. It goes on. It all depends on the land ...

Mr Everingham waited two and a half weeks before he outlined his intention to 'help Aboriginal people feel some involvement with decisions taken about Ayers Rock'. The proposal for traditional owners to lease the area to the Australian National Parks Service was not part of his plan. He wanted Ayers Rock to be administered by the Territory Parks and Wildlife Commission, successors to the Reserves Board which had taken the Rock over when it was removed from the Petermann Reserve (Melbourne *Sun* and *The Canberra Times*, 27 April 1979). The meeting itself took place on 9 May, a week after Neville Perkins, the region's representative in the Northern Territory Legislative Assembly, had publicly reiterated the traditional owners' undertaking not to hinder tourism, and again called on the Federal Government to give them title so that the traditional owners could

have the same standing as the Aboriginal landowners of Kakadu (*Centralian Advocate*, 3 May 1979). It transpired that all Everingham had to offer was one-third representation on the Park's board of management (*Adelaide Advertiser*, 12 May 1979), a proposal that came nowhere near what the traditional owners wanted. Unfortunately, the Federal Government had again lost interest in the issue. In September, when the outcome of the remainder of the claim was announced, Wenten Rabuntja said that no decision had yet been made about title to the Park: 'Mr Fraser told us he understood how important the land was to Aborigines and Senator Chaney said he would bring the matter before the Government. But we are still waiting' (*Northern Territory News*, 26 October 1979).

Towards the end of November, Neville Perkins wrote to the Prime Minister asking again for Uluru and Katatjuta to be returned to their traditional owners in the same manner as the Kakadu National Park, but to no effect (*Northern Territory News*, 21 November 1979). Title remained with the Director of the Australian National Parks and Wildlife Service.

The land claim outside the National Park

Following the Commissioner's ruling on the status of the National Park, the Aboriginal claimants were left with an area of peripheral country to which their claim could be heard. Forming an inverted L in shape, the area runs from Lake Amadeus to the edge of the Mulga Park pastoral lease (Figure 6). It contains no permanent water other than the brackish natural spring at Katiti. The adjoining base camps lie either on pastoral leases (Atila and Aputjilpi), in the National Park (Uluru and Katatjuta) or more distantly, in the Petermann Reserve (Kulpitjata and Apara). Apart from Katiti, sites in the claim area consist of one normally dry creek bed draining from Katatjuta, called Karu Wilula, and four widely scattered soaks and rock holes: Tjilpil, Yularanya Pulka, Yularanya Tjukutjuku and Wakuliyannga. The claim also took in the south-eastern end of Pantu, Lake Amadeus, which consists of salt and black mud. Given the wording of the Land Rights Act, evidence for the ownership of the 5360 square kilometres of sandhill and mulga flat that remained in the claim depended on establishing which Aboriginal groups primarily held spiritual responsibility for these seven places, and how the land-owning groups were composed.

Because of their peripheral nature, all seven sites lie in areas where the edges of adjacent estates overlap. The claim was further complicated by the fact that this was the first time in which membership of the land-owning groups was not exclusively handed down from father to son; for the first time, some people gave evidence that they could inherit membership of their mother's group.

Although the Act was carefully worded to reflect Aboriginal principles of land ownership, the wording is inevitably not the sort Aboriginal people generally use. Moreover, it usually takes an anthropologist many months to discover how the society he or she is studying really works. None of us, unless specially trained, could fully describe our own society to a foreigner, and anthropologists spend many hours recording how people behave as well as asking direct questions before they are ready to describe a society. To understand, for instance, how people carried out 'primary spiritual responsibilities', it would be important to see them at ceremonies, not just to ask them to talk about what they do. Although the Aboriginal Land Commissioner has attended ceremonies and visited sacred sites with the traditional owners, there is simply not the time for him, at a hearing, to carry out all his own research. The Aboriginal evidence at Uluru was given over five days and included a visit to parts of Yulara. An attempt was made to reach Purrarra Well, but recent rain had made the intervening salt pans uncrossable (a photograph of this expedition published by the Commissioner on page 32 of his report tactfully conceals the fact that one vehicle has been bogged down near the edge of the pan). Again, while Pitjantjatjara and Yankuntjatjara can talk about handing on their mother's and father's countries, they do not have any technical terms to describe the special features of their system. Only

Peter Bulla, who had lived with Aranda at Hermannsburg and Jay Creek, could describe how the predominantly patrilineal system of the Aranda worked. The Commissioner must, therefore, fit together the various statements by witnesses in their evidence and use the special procedures developed by courts of justice to test the validity of evidence: the right of lawyers representing other parties to cross-examine witnesses, the rule that hearsay evidence (talking about what one has been told by others, rather than one's own experience) is not allowed, and so forth. Fortunately the Commissioner already had considerable experience of working with Aboriginal people in court, and understood the particular problems they have in speaking freely under such stressful circumstances.

One of the problems facing Aboriginal people in land claims is understanding the difference between giving evidence and traditional Aboriginal ways of teaching people about their society. Before they give evidence, the lawyers and anthropologists practise the questions to be asked, to make sure the questions are straightforward and understandable, and to make sure they know what the answers will be. Since Aboriginal people are expected to remember what they have been taught, the witnesses found it difficult to understand why, when they went into the hearing, the same lawyer asked the same questions, in order to let the Commissioner hear the evidence.

As the interpreter explained at one point, 'they are just saying they have got all that, why do we have to go through it again'. Sometimes witnesses will conclude that the lawyer wants further information on the same subject, as when one woman, asked to list the owners of an estate, racked her brain to recall the names of children she had not mentioned before, rather than repeat the senior members she had named outside the hearing. There is no doubt that, for these reasons, some of the evidence was confusing. The Commissioner comments in his report on the dramatic change in numbers of claimants as the case progressed (Toohey 1980, p.4), and on the fact that 'the process of extracting information in order to piece together the responsibility of a land owning group can be a difficult one'.

Listening to the Aboriginal evidence, for instance, I realised that the lists of places belonging to estates that I had collected during my fieldwork (see, for instance, the lists for Uluru in Chapter 3), were not ones that the speakers had learned like multiplication tables. They were thinking them out, as they spoke, on the basis of their lifetime's experience. When they said, for instance, 'Puntitjata belongs to Aputjilpinya because we used to go there from Aputjilpi', or 'Yulara belongs to Uluru because we always went there after rain', it was clear that they were thinking about a country (estate) as an area focused on a permanent water but including

Figure 6
Location of area
defined in land
claim.

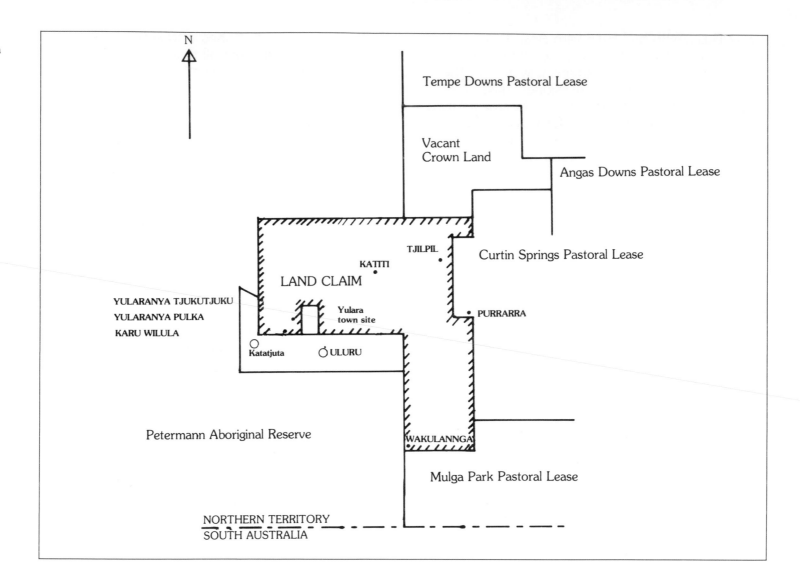

N

Tempe Downs Pastoral Lease

Vacant
Crown Land

Angas Downs Pastoral Lease

TJILPIL

Curtin Springs Pastoral Lease

KATITI

LAND CLAIM

YULARANYA TJUKUTJUKU
YULARANYA PULKA
KARU WILULA

Yulara
town site

PURRARRA

Katatjuta ☿ULURU

Petermann Aboriginal Reserve

WAKULANNGA

Mulga Park Pastoral Lease

NORTHERN TERRITORY
SOUTH AUSTRALIA

peripheral waters as far as those accessible from other base camps. When, on the other hand, people said Yulara belonged to Katatjuta because the dreaming track came from Katatjuta, it is clear they were thinking in terms of *ngura inma nguru*, 'country from the songs' (*see* Chapter 3). Because of this, members of adjacent estates sometimes both claimed ownership of certain peripheral sites, and there were inconsistencies of detail between different lists. From the list of nineteen sites Aboriginal witnesses attributed to the estate centred on Katatjuta, five also appear in the list of places later attributed to the Uluru estate. Another site was explicitly said to be shared by the two estates. The fact that the land claimed contained only peripheral soaks and rock holes focused attention on these discrepancies. Whether or not sites were said to be shared depended to some extent on the form of the question. To answer, 'Which places belong to Uluru?' it would not necessarily be relevant to say that some such places also belonged to another estate. The broader question, 'Who sings the songs for Wakuliyannga?'—a peripheral site on the Mala track between Uluru and Aputjilpi—is likely to evoke a general answer such as 'everyone' or 'we all do', because this kind of question reminds people of shared ritual responsibility.

It was not always crucial to discover which group held the primary interest in a site, because the groups holding both Uluru and Katatjuta were proved to hold primary responsibility for other places in the claim area. Claimants from Atila and Apara were not so fortunate, owing to the lack of evidence that they held, or shared, primary responsibility for any site on the claim area.

Purrarra is, physically, closer to Atila than Uluru and was generally described to me as on the edge of Atila Country. In evidence, Toby Nangina said that Purrarra belonged to Uluru (transcript pp.570 and 632); Nipper Winmati later stated that it belonged to both Uluru and Atila (p.729). Asked who starts the songs for Purrarra, Winmati answered that he sang them as far as Purrarra, after which a senior Atila man took over (pp.730–1). Nyinnga Stewart, an Atila man, said that Purrarra should belong to Ayers Rock but, asked whether the Atila men also held country around that place, replied that they did (p.731). The Commissioner accepted that there was some evidence Purrarra was shared by the Atila estate (Toohey 1980, p.16), but unfortunately for the claimants, the boundary of Curtin Springs pastoral lease makes a deviation to include this valuable natural spring, and it is about 1 kilometre inside the edge of the lease.

Tjilpil, the nearest site within the claim to Purrarra, was first identified as Ayers Rock country by Toby Nangina, but later he appears to say that it belongs to both Atila ('his country') and Uluru (p.732). He went on, however, to say that no dreaming figure stopped at Tjilpil. Winmati said no one looked after the place; people simply used it as a camp on hunting expeditions. He and Bill Ukai explained that you cannot camp at Tjilpil for more than one night because the water is too salt. The Commissioner, while accepting that Tjilpil lay within the claim area, was not satisfied that members of the Atila estate had any primary spiritual responsibility for it. Indeed, if no dreaming is associated with it, it is difficult to see how any group could hold spiritual responsibility for the place.

Katiti is a site linked to Apara by the track of the Wanampi who made Aparanya Creek, his route diving underground where the creek drains into the sandhills and re-emerging on the shore of Lake Amadeus (see Chapters 1 and 2). The Apara claimants gave evidence of this dreaming track (transcript pp.708–9). Nipper Winmati said Katiti belonged to Uluru and Katatjuta, but Apara had a story for the place (p.732A): he and Pompy Douglas related part of the story, but said there were no songs associated with it (p.732B). The Commissioner ruled that while the members of the Apara estate had claimed an association with Katiti, they had not demonstrated they held or shared primary spiritual responsibility for it (Toohey 1980, p.15), and they could not be recognised as traditional owners of part of the claim area. In the end, only Uluru, Katatjuta and Aputjilpi (the latter shares responsibility for Wakuliyannga) were found to hold sites in the claim area.

Paradoxically, evidence of spiritual responsibility can also be hard to establish for the most sacred places, because Aboriginal law puts witnesses under considerable constraint not to reveal the most significant part of belief or ceremony. Probably in all land claims claimants have decided that, however much they want to win recognition of their title, there is a point beyond which they will not divulge the full significance of certain sites. Recognising this, the Commissioner has always allowed some evidence to be heard in restricted sessions, although even this cannot remove all restraint. In the Ayers Rock claim witnesses for Katatjuta would not explain the relevance of some sites to ceremony, while one witness for Uluru declined to answer a question on the grounds that whatever he answered he would reveal the existence of ceremonial secrets.

On the question of constructing the estate from the evidence of responsibility for particular sites, the Commissioner found no problem, writing that, 'there is no doubt that the notion of estates was familiar to the claimants. Many witnesses spoke of their country as Katatjuta or Ayers Rock or one of the other named estates' and just as readily identified the estates to which their mothers and fathers had belonged (1980, pp.5–6).

The constitution of the local descent group—the group sharing primary spiritual responsibility for sites in the estate—was a little more problematic (this is discussed in Layton 1983b). Despite this, it was clear from what Aboriginal witnesses said that membership of estates did not have to be taken from one's father, and that Pitjantjatjara and Yankuntjatjara descent groups were not the patrilineal units known from other parts of Aboriginal Australia. The Commissioner cited a number of examples from the evidence.

As in other claims, there proved to be no difficulty in showing that the descent group was entitled to forage in its own estate. As the Commissioner wrote, 'evidence of this emerged at every turn' (1980, p.16; the evidence is summarised on the following page of his report at paragraph 104).

Considering the claimants' strength of traditional attachment to the land claimed, the Commissioner agreed that this was strong. He referred to the distance people had travelled to attend the hearings and the readiness of Aboriginal people from the audience to join in while others were giving evidence. During visits to Uluru and the claim area, 'the attitude of people at sites ... where songs and stories, very much part of the land, were recounted showed great enthusiasm' (1980, p.25). The reluctance of witnesses to speak about particular sites and dreamings of special importance was also expressive of their strong traditional attachment. The Commissioner did not find much evidence of a desire to live on the claim area, but acknowledged that this was because

once Uluru and Katatjuta were excluded from the claim, the remaining country was not very suitable for living on; indeed, it contains no traditional base camp. 'As so often happens,' the Commissioner wrote, 'the unalienated Crown Land available to be claimed is the harshest country in the area' (p.26). Napala Jack spoke of moving out to Yularanya Tjuku Tjuku to collect food after rain, and this is how the land was used during the period of the subsistence economy. In the light of evidence for the existence of traditional ownership, strength of attachment and desire to live on the land, the Commissioner recommended in his report to the Minister that the claim should succeed.

He found it difficult to measure how many people would benefit, since a full assessment of those with traditional attachment to the land would require a detailed consideration of dreaming tracks and of relationships to the land, which would be far beyond the scope of the claim, but he accepted that it would number several hundred people. More importantly, witnesses from the Pitjantjatjara Council had spoken about their efforts to gain recognition of land rights in South and Western Australia, and the claimants had been unable to have their case for traditional ownership of the Uluru National Park heard. The Commissioner argued that recognition of traditional title to the land claimed would thus be an advantage both to the claimants and to the wider Pitjantjatjara community, summarising his comments:

> The advantages of a grant lie mainly in the recognition of traditional ownership for members of a tribal group engaged in trying to secure a wider recognition when the land of greatest significance is not available to be claimed under the Act'. (p.31)

He was impressed by the importance Uluru and Katatjuta held for Aboriginal witnesses. Both were shown to be of enormous significance, not only to those responsible for them in Aboriginal law, but also to the claimants generally and a wider range of Aboriginal people. Witnesses had sometimes spoken about them almost to the exclusion of other sites and country (1980, p.10).

Detriment, on the other hand, would be minimal. Once it was established that the National Park could not be claimed, all the objectors who would have argued a detriment to the Australian community in general, or to tourism in particular, withdrew. Four parties had some mining interest in parts of the original claim area, but none gave any evidence that the claim as granted would affect them.

The Commissioner's report was presented to the Minister for Aboriginal Affairs on 31 August 1979. On 11 October the Minister announced that, after consulting with the Northern Territory Government, he had accepted the Report and would recommend to the Governor-General that title to the claim area be given to the Aboriginal Land Trust that he would establish.

Although they failed to gain legal recognition of Aboriginal title to the National Park, the claimants had achieved a considerable victory. Through an exacting legal inquiry, they had established their ownership of the adjacent country, so that the National Park was now completely surrounded by Aboriginal land. This alone would have made it hard to believe there were not Aboriginal people who, in their law, owned the country within the arbitrary Park boundaries. More specifically, the Aboriginal Land Commissioner found that there do exist estates centred on Uluru and Katatjuta, and he identified the people who belong to them. The object of the hearing then became, as he described it, to assess 'the extent to which those estates have responsibility beyond the immediate vicinity of Uluru and Katatjuta' (1980, p.10). Since it was the sites within the National Park that were demonstrated to be of most significance to claimants, it is inconceivable that, having proved their traditional ownership of peripheral sites on the claim area, they could not also have proved their ownership of the parts of their estates that fall inside the Park, had that land not been taken by the Australian National Parks Service.

I have heard people, particularly people with tourist interests at Uluru, publicly claim that no living Aboriginal involvement in the Rock survives: the rich associations of legend that they point out to tourists are said to belong to the past, not the present. Such people have also suggested that, if Aboriginal people do survive who have an association with Uluru, then they are merely a handful of old men. At a slide-show in one of the motels, for instance, 'Captain' Ikuta was identified in a photograph as 'one of the last of the Pitjantjatjara', a claim that ignores the existence of 1700 people belonging to the Pitjantjatjara, Yankuntjatjara and related dialect groups living at Ernabella, Docker River and in neighbouring communities. There are, of course, progressively fewer left of those who grew up in the days of the purely hunting and gathering economy, but the sense of Aboriginal identity among younger people is strong and the handing-on of knowledge continues.

It was argued in the press, in the year following the claim, that because Bill Harney had allegedly found it hard to elicit details of the stories about Uluru from the old men with whom he worked, there really was little knowledge left of these stories. This is simply not true; in fact, what Harney did learn agrees well with what C.P. Mountford, and later I, were told. It was also argued that Aboriginal religion was a primitive cult, and so it had no right to impede economic 'progress'. The logic of this argument depends on the notion that, because Aboriginal people were until recently hunters and gatherers, their religion has survived undeveloped from the early period of human development. But we have no more

knowledge about early Aboriginal religion than we have about that of their contemporaries, our own hunting and gathering ancestors. What is certain is that modern Aboriginal religion in the desert is the inspiration of the desert people's determination today to hold onto, and respect, their unique culture. Sacred sites are only a pointer to the complex philosophy embodied in that religion, but it is one to which the land is all important. An agreement between the Aboriginal owners and the Australian National Parks Service like that operating at Kakadu would have recognised the owners' battle over the last fifty years to keep their links with the sacred sites of Uluru and Katatjuta.

In June 1982, the Federal Government offered to recognise the prior ownership of Uluru by Aboriginal people in an agreement that would declare the area a National Park under Northern Territory legislation. Unfortunately this offer was part of a package that included amendments to the Land Rights Act that would prevent Aboriginal groups from applying to have pastoral properties to which they held the lease converted to Aboriginal land. Although the amendment did not directly concern the Aboriginal owners of Uluru, they rejected the changes. As Nipper Winmati and others put it, 'Country is sacred to all Aboriginals and we are very sad that you want us to get our country by climbing all over those Aranda, Warlpiri and others in the north' (*Central Australian Land Rights News*, June–July 1982, p.4).

The original drafting of a Land Rights Act was undertaken by a Labor government, and it was not until a new Labor government came to power that Aboriginal title to Uluru was finally acknowledged on 11 November 1983. An agreement along the lines of that governing administration of the Kakadu park was announced. 'This', said the new Prime Minister, Mr Hawke, 'is an historic decision and is a measure of the willingness of this Government on behalf of the Australian people, to recognise the just and legitimate claims of a people who have been dispossessed of their land, but who have never lost their spiritual attachment to that land'.

Half a century after their first serious encounter with White settlers, and twenty-five years after Uluru had been excised from their reserve, the Aboriginal owners fianlly won legal recognition of their status.

As the Governor General fittingly concluded in his speech of 26 October 1985 when handing title deeds to the traditional owners, both Uluru and Katatjuta have, through the sense of awe and wonder they create, a very special significance for all Australians. 'For many Aboriginal people,' he continued, 'this place has still deeper meaning and deep spiritual significance, a significance whose roots go back to time immemorial. And now, today, the Uluru–Katatjuta Aboriginal Land Trust becomes the custodian of this heartland of Australia. The Trust, by the Deed which is to be handed over today, acquires inaliable freehold title under Australian law to this place which is so special to its members. At the same time, recognizing, too, the special significance of Uluru to *all* Australians, and the appropriateness of its remaining as a National Park.'

A comparison of Mountford's and Harney's accounts of the main sites at Uluru

Place name	Harney (1968)	Mountford (1977)
Mala Story		
Katji tilkil	paragraph 19, p.13	'Kadidi' (not associated with Mala, according to Mountford), pp.20, 32, 132, and 135–6
Tjunku Urrpu	'Djungaba', paragraph 20, p.13	p.68
Mala Puta	'The Puta', paragraph 23, p.13	—
Walputi	'The Nowamara', paragraph 28, p.15	—
Tjukutjapi	'Dundajabbi', paragraph 32, p.15	pp.67 and 107
Inintitjara	'Inindi', paragraph 34, pp. 15 and 17; paragraph 37, p.19	'Tjinindi', pp.108–9, 114 and 146–8
Taputji	'Tuppudji', paragraph 38, p.19	'Tabudja', pp.74–8
Kuniya Story		
Waraiyuki	'Worreaki', paragraph 29, p.15	pp.86 incl. n. 15, 96
Ngunaliri	'Ninjerri', paragraph 30, p.15. Snake incorrectly identified as tree goanna	p.68
Kuniya Piti	paragraph 17, p.13	'Kunia Piti', pp.60–4
Wila Alpuru	'Lagari, the laughter cave' paragraph 13, p.11	—
Untju Kuntanya	'Kudjuk Kundunda', paragraph 5, p.9 and plate 15 (wrongly located)	'mouth of mourning Kunia', p.55
Uluru rock hole	'Uluru', p.7	p.154
Mutitjulu	'Mutidjula', paragraphs 8, p.9, and 10–12, p.11	'Mutitjilda', pp.48, 50, 52, 54 and 56
Alyurungu	'Owwilitti', paragraph 1, p.9	pp.40 and 44
Walu Kutjuta	—	pp.40 and 42

Place name	Harney (1968)	Mountford (1977)
Mita and Lungkata Story		
Kurumpa	'Kirrimbirr' (not Mita and Lungkata, according to Harney), and paragraph 2, p.9	pp.137–8
Kalaiya Tjunta	'Djundi', paragraph 14, p.11	pp.137–8
Mita Kampantja (*Mita Kampantja*, Mita's ashes, is also known as *Lungkata Waru*, Lungkata's fire)	'Meta Camba', paragraph 2, p.9	pp.140, 142 and 144
Pulari Story		
Pulari	'Bularri', paragraph 4, p.9	'Bulari', pp.40 and 45–7
Tjati Story		
Walaritja	paragraph 27, p.15	caption to plate 74 and p.120
Kantju	'Kundju', paragraph 27, p.15	'Kandju', pp.114 and 120
Itjaritjari		
Itjaritjarilpa	paragraph 21, p.13	pp.126, 129–32

Pitjantjatjara and Yankuntjatjara place names

Aboriginal named places are the most convenient units through which to build up an understanding of land use and land ownership.* All the complementary and cross-cutting categories, such as ancestral tracks, stretches of country subject to ownership by descent groups, or ecological zones, can be defined when Aboriginal people cite the appropriate place names. When these places are located on the map, then the categories under consideration can be drawn in. The sharp geological divide separating the Quarternary alluvium of creek outwashes and sand dunes or alluvial flats from the ancient sandstone, gneiss and granite of the hills in central Australia generally makes the geological map a more accurate record of topography than the topographic map itself. It is frequently useful also to refer to air photos to locate smaller natural features.

The bush is dotted with named places; the name may be that of a hill (*puli*), cave (*kulpi*), creek (*karu*), or water source. There is, for instance, a small isolated hill at the eastern end of the Petermann Ranges called Puli Pultanya (SG52-7 298863). This hill lies a short distance from the east bank of Armstrong Creek, and the creek's Pitjantjatjara name is Karu Pultanya, a name which extends to a point 20 kilometres further north, where the creek is crossed by the road to Docker River. Mutitjulu water (Maggie's Spring) on the south side of Uluru is called Kapi Mutitjulu, while the large rockshelter at the foot of the western cliff 200 metres from the water is sometimes called Kulpi Mutitjulu. A hill is often named from one of the water sources at its foot, and stretches of creek bed likewise frequently are known by the name of a reliable source of water within that section. Different sections of the same creek may have different names.

Where it can be translated, the place name generally refers to the natural features of the site, or to its mythological associations. Since mythology often gains expression in natural features, these two sources are not necessarily independent. One example of a name referring to a natural feature is Karu Kali (A *kali* is a bent throwing stick), which is the name of a winding section of the Hull River east of Docker River Community (SG52-3 222893 and for about 10 kilometres downstream). Another such name is Karutjara (creek-having), which is a waterhole south of Mount Currie, near the old road to Giles Meterological Station (SG52-8 360871). Arrnguli-arrnguli, a small hill adjacent to the Docker River road (SG52-7 272883) takes its name from the *arrnguli* wild plum that grows there; Pinala Kutjara (Two Ears) from the conical outline of the two small hills so named (at SG52-8 404804 and 403803) in the sandhill country north-east of Kulpitjata.

The spur on the south-east face of Uluru where the lizards Lungkata and Mita buried the thigh of their stolen emu is called Kalaiya Tjunta, or Emu Thigh. Kungka Mana (Girl's Buttock), a hill at the entrance to a passage through the northern tip of the Musgrave Ranges (at SG52-8 398788) acquired its name because a heroine of the dreaming sat there during the creation period.

In some instances, two or more places have the same name. There is a Piltati in the Petermann Ranges and another, visited by C.P. Mountford, in the Mann Range west of Amata; there is a Kungka Mana near Docker River, which gives its name to the Mannanana (Mananya) Range east of the settlement.

Some Aboriginal place names are recorded on the 1:250000 topographic maps; others have been documented by explorers and travellers, and this documentation is

---

*My appreciation of the techniques involved, and the usefulness of mapping named places, came from work with Athol Chase and Peter Sutton in Cape York, during September–October 1974. The technique had been considerably developed by John von Sturmer and Athol Chase during their previous research in North Queensland.

summarised below. In some cases, the name of a particular place is extended to refer to surrounding country which includes other, less important, sites. The principal usage of this kind, to refer to estates, is discussed in Chapter 3. In one instance, that of Kikingkura, the name is further extended to refer to a cluster of adjacent estates including Kikingkura proper, Puntitjata and Untulyu (their approximate location is shown in Figure 5).

Records of Aboriginal place names in the Uluru region

Anari (SG52–8 494825)

A spring south-west of Atila, Anari is the site of the now abandoned Mount Conner homestead. M. Terry visited it on his way to the Petermann Ranges in 1930, recording the name as Oneri. He described it as 'a seemingly permanent limestone well'. Although this was before the construction of the homestead, the well had already been deepened to provide water for stock by, Terry believed, the Baileys of Erldunda (Terry n.d., p.26). Strehlow mentions the site in his account of Kai-Umen's execution, writing it 'Aneri' (Strehlow 1970, pp.120–1). Mountford camped there in 1940 on his way to Ayers Rock, and he recorded the name as 'Anneri'. He wrote down the legendary fight between the two boys of the Tjukurrpa that happened here (Mountford 1950, p.75; see also Groom 1950, pp.182–8). The name appears as Aneri Well on the topographic map.

Apara (SG52–12 407766)

This site was often visited by White parties travelling to the Mann or Petermann Ranges. Because it was a reliable source of water it became a popular point for doggers to collect dingo scalps from Aboriginal groups, and at one time it was considered as a site for the mission eventually established at Ernabella (Duguid 1972, p.121). F.R. George records the name as 'Opparinna'; this is Aparanya, the *-nya*

ending is a locative suffix frequently attached to names when they refer to places (Basedow 1914, pp.94, 96–100 and 160–5: plates 12, 43 and 44). D. Mackay records the name as 'Abarra' (1929, p.264 and map). H.H. Finlayson (1935, p.44) describes how two men directed him there, and he uses the spelling later adopted by Mountford, 'Oparinna' (1950, p.137). Oparinna Creek is marked on the topographic maps.

Atila (Mount Conner)

The name Attila appears in the police records concerning the execution of Kai-Umen (AA19), as do Eraka (Iyarrka) and Ilanula.

Ituntu (SG52–7 254885)

Ituntu is a soak at the foot of a ridge where the Docker River road cuts through the Petermann Ranges between Shaw Creek and Chirnside Creek. The name is extended to the ridge itself. Mackay recorded the name in his account of the 1926 expedition (1929, p.263), writing that they were joined by a group of four Aboriginal people here who went southward with them up the course of Irving Creek and the next day showed them a soak called 'Tortarinna'. Mackay's (or Basedow's) transcription of the name is Etundu. Etundu Ridge is shown on the map accompanying Mackay's paper, and in larger scale on Basedow's map in the Australian Archives.

Iyarrka (SG52–8 494852)

This is a spring 10.5 kilometres east of Curtin Springs homestead. On the topographic map it is called Spring Well, but W.E. Harney refers to it as 'Yerka' in the account of his arrival at Uluru to work as ranger (1969, p.41). It was the original site of Curtin Springs homestead. See also Atila entry, above.

Katatjuta (the Olgas)

This name first appears on Basedow's map recording the

route of the Wells Expedition (1914). In the records of Kai-Umen's execution it is written 'Cutta Toota', as in the statement of Kai-Umen's widow, Judy: 'Kai-Umen belong to Cutta Toota and I belong to Cutta Toota too' (AA20).

Katiti (SG52–8 425887)

Katiti is a natural spring 9 kilometres south of Pantu, Lake Amadeus—the name is first recorded by Baldwin Spencer and F.J. Gillen (1912, p.111) in 1894, who visited it on their way to Uluru and transcribed the name Kurtitina (Katitinya). On Basedow's map of the 1903 Wells Expedition, it is marked 'Curtyteena' (1914). The topographic map calls it Bobbie's Well.

Kikingkura

This is the reference place for the estate in which the Docker River Community is now located. The Pitjantjatjara name was first recorded by the Mackay expedition of 1926, where it is rather quaintly transcribed as Mount Kikinguana (Kikingkuranya). Terry, who in 1930 used Giles's map with additions from the Mackay expedition's material, makes the rather obvious joke that his party rechristened it Mount Kicking Goanna. Harney gets the sound right when he calls the place Kikingurra (1969, p.168). He and Peter Severin made an expedition through the Petermann Ranges in 1962, shortly before Harney's death. They were accompanied by Tjuwirri and another man whose countries lay in the area, although at that time there were no permanent residents around Docker River.

Mananya (SG52–3 191903)

Mananya is the name of the ridge in the Petermann Ranges running east from Docker River. The site from which the ridge takes its name lies at its western end, and the whole ridge is part of Kikingkura country. The Mackay expedition recorded the name as 'Mannanana', but Basedow's map compiled from the expedition applies it to the range

between Kikingkura and the Hull River and his identification is followed by the modern topographic map. This section of the ridge is more accurately called Tjuntinya, after the place where it is bounded by the Hull River.

Mungkuwara (SG52–7 285862)

Mungkuwara is the most easterly hill in the Petermann Ranges. It lies 3.5 kilometres north-east of Giles's Mount McCulloch, on the west side of Karu Pultanya, Armstrong Creek. On the east side of the creek, the more scattered hills of the Olia Chain begin. Mackay describes how two Aboriginal men accompanied the 1926 expedition from 'Tortarinna Spring' to Mount McCulloch, and how he and Basedow climbed the hill: 'We had a magnificent view from here over the Pottoyu Hills (to the south), and also of the hill that terminates the Petermann Range–Mount Mungoranna' (1929, p.263). On Basedow's map, Mungoranna (Mungkuwaranya) is shown due east of Mount McCulloch. It is possible that they have confused Mount McCulloch with Giles's Mount Phillips. Mackay records the Pitjantjatjara name for Mount McCulloch is Nangorru. My compass bearings on the hill called Nangkurrnga strongly suggested that it was the hill the topographic map identifies as Mount Phillips. Nangkurr, Mungkawara and Alukata (SG52–7 291863) are all in Piltati country.

Piki

Piki is a spring on the northern side of Pantu (Lake Amadeus). This is apparently the place F.R. George calls 'Piggirra' in his diary entry for 22 February 1906.

Piltati (SG52–7 circa 274867)

Piltati is the reference point for one of the Petermann estates. It should not be confused with a second Piltati, of which Mountford and Tindale have written, in the Mann Ranges. This is the country to which the father of

Tjalkalyiri, Napala and Peter Bulla belonged. Like Apara in the Musgrave Ranges, Piltati was known to early White travellers as a reliable water source, so features in a number of accounts. Mackay went there from Nangkurr: 'After circling round some hills about 6 miles and turning north-west we came to Piltadinnya water, at the base of a quartzite gorge where there was a natural reservoir and, some 20 feet higher up, two fine rock holes containing a large supply of water' (1929, p.263). When Terry's party visited the water four years later, they found their way to it by following a 'well-marked camel pad' (n.d., p.42). His description closely matches Mackay's. He includes a photograph of the site (Terry n.d., facing p.43), and one of the view from the hill above, taken next to a cairn constructed by earlier visitors (facing p.52). W. Gill went to Piltati in 1931. He could see no sign of Aboriginal people having been there in the 'appreciable past', but found 'ample evidence left by the few White men' who had been there before (1968, pp.81–2). In 1939, when T.G.H. Strehlow and C. Duguid travelled to the Petermann Ranges, Strehlow selected Piltati as a meeting point to collect camels brought from Hermannsburg. Strehlow published a photograph of Piltati, perhaps taken on this expedition, in his paper on *Culture, Social Structure and Environment in Central Australia* (1965, facing p.134). I have not visited the site, and the location I have given here is based on compass bearings.

Pulpaiyala

This is a soak marking the spot from which the *mamu* was dispatched by the Wintalka men of Kikingkura to punish the Wati Mala at Uluru. Harney refers to it in his account of the expedition he and Peter Severin undertook in the early 1960s. Harney describes how Tjuwirri gave them the name and talked of the 'ritual dog Kuapunni' (Kurrpanngu) (1969, p.168). He spells the name both as 'Pupialla' and,

more accurately, 'Pulpialla' (1969, pp.168–75). The site is close to the present Kikingkura outstation.

Puntitjara (SG52–8 448797)

Puntitjara is one of the few sites in the Kelly Hills whose name is recorded by early White travellers. Basedow camped near there in 1903; 'About two miles E. of this camp, Immalangenna disclosed to us a small, but good, native soakage-well existing in a fissure within the finely foliated gneiss, at about five feet from the surface ... The native name of the soakage is Punndijarrinna' (1914, p.173). Basedow published photographs, one of three men, one of three women and four children, whom his party met here (plate 47, facing p.172). Strehlow evidently visited Puntitjara during the 1930s, because in the first part of his account of Aboriginal mythology in the *Inland Review* he published a photograph of 'A Jankuntjatjara hunter from a party met at Puntitjara soak, Kelly Hills on August 11th, 1936' (1969b, p.13). The soak belongs to the Kelly Hills estate, Aputjilpi.

Puta-puta (SG52–7 250881)

Puta-puta is a soak in the Petermann Ranges, on the creek Giles called the Chirnside. It lies a short distance south of the present Docker River road crossing and provides the reference place for the estate between Kikingkura and Pilati, the estate to which Imalangu (Harry Bigfoot) and his brother Pinganti are primarily affiliated. In 1931, Gill was accompanied by several people from a large camp he encountered on the Hull River, to the soak itself, which he calls Putta Putta Springs (1968, p.159). Harney, in his account of the expedition to the Petermanns, refers to crossing 'the sandy creek of Mowanyu [Muwanya, Giles's Shaw Creek] ... and, fourteen miles further on, the Armstrong or "Puta-puta" river of the Petermann Aborigines' (1969, p.166). Muwa is in Puta-puta country.

Tjulu (SG52–8 483853)

This, the present site of Curtin Springs homestead, is mentioned by Harney (1969, p.63). (The reference is quoted in Chapter 5.)

Uluru

Uluru is first recorded on Basedow's map compiled during the Wells expedition of 1903 (1914). The police records of Kai-Umen's execution in 1935 and the ensuing trial refer to it a number of times. Several of the Aboriginal people involved, including Paddy Uluru, identify it as their country (AA21).

Aboriginal use of natural resources in and adjacent to claim area during period of fieldwork

Plants used—names and habitats

Aboriginal name	Common English name	Botanical name
Steep rock face (*apu* = rocky outcrop)		
ilyi	rock fig	Ficus platypoda
kupata	wild plum	Santalum lanceolatum
mingkulpa	wild tobacco	Nicotiana gossei
urtjanpa	spear bush	Pandorea doratoxylon
Hill slopes (*puli* = hill, *puliku ngura* = hilly country)		
utjalpara	—	Acacia ammobia
kulipura (Pitjantjatjara)	'Christmas' tree	Callitris glauca
walngati (Yankuntjatjara)	'Christmas' tree	Callitris glauca
Eucalpyt zones (*itara* = bloodwood; *itara-itara* = bloodwood country)		
(y)itara	bloodwood	Eucalyptus termanilis
wakati	—	Portulaca oleracea
kunakanti	—	Brachiaria miliformis
?	bush tomato	Solanum elipticum
Mulga flats (*puti* = witchetty grub; *putitjara* or *putingka* = 'grub' country; mulga zone)		
wintalka	mulga seeds	—
wanari (Pitjantjatjara)	mulga tree	Acacia aneura
kurrkurr (Yankuntjatjara)	mulga tree	Acacia aneura
ilpilati	Ayers Rock mulga	Acacia ayersiana
ilkuwara	witchetty bush	Acacia kempeana
wangunu	wooly-butt grass	Eragrostis eriopida or E. laniflora
kaltu-kaltu	native millet	Panicum decompositum
mintingka	eremophila	Eremophila latrobei

Aboriginal name	Common English name	Botanical name
Sandhills (*tali* = sandhill; *taliku ngura* = sandhill country; *kurrkara* = desert oak; *kurrkara-kurrkara* = desert oak country)		
kurrkara	desert oak	*Casuarina decaisneana*
walkalpa	emu poison bush	*Duboisia hopwoodii*
kalingkaling	—	*Grevillea eriostachya*
untulyu	—	*Gyrostemon ramulosus*
ilpara	water bush	*Grevillea nematophylla*
arrnguli	wild plum	*Santalum lanceolatum*
kampurrapa	wild tomato	*Solanum centrale*
kiti	(gum from) spinifex	*Triodia basedowii*
unturrngu	wild banana	*Leichhardtia australis*
kanturangu (Pitjantjatjara)	desert poplar	*Codonocarpus cotinifolius*
kaluti (Yankuntjatjara)	desert poplar	*Codonocarpus cotinifolius*

*Peter Fannin, of the Northern Territory Parks and Wildlife Service at Uluru, kindly provided me with many botanical identifications. Many species have already been documented by, for example, Silberbauer (1971), Gould (1969 and 1971) and Peterson (1978).

Subsistence activities observed

During fieldwork at Ayers Rock I worked primarily with Paddy Uluru and his household. Throughout the period there were several other family groups living at the Rock, and they undoubtedly engaged in subsistence activities that I failed to observe. The incidents documented below probably represent less than 50 per cent of the total.

Fieldwork September to December 1977

3 October Paddy Uluru goes out on foot from Bore 29 camp to obtain wood for manufacturing boomerangs from mulga trees.

6 October Paddy Uluru driven south from the Rock at his request to hunt for red kangaroo (unsuccessfully), in the Petermann Reserve.

25 October During visit to Utiti, on western border of National Park, Napala Jack, Tjalkalyiri, Wintjin Walkabout and Paddy Uluru dig for witchetty grubs and cut wood to manufacture boomerangs.

27 October Paddy Uluru cuts wood from spear bush trees at Walpanya (in Olgas) to make light spears; exchanges some lengths immediately for cigarettes from party of tourists.

29 October Wintjin Walkabout cuts wood from spear-bushes at Walpanya.

30 October Paddy Uluru goes on foot from Bore 29 camp and shoots two red kangaroo.

14 November Paddy Uluru and his son Albie shoot rabbits in vacant Crown Land north of Olgas.

20 November   Paddy Uluru and Albie cut wood for boomerangs from mulga trees in Park east of Ayers Rock.

22 November   Mary and Eileen Captain collect firewood at the Olgas, while Cassidy and Albie Uluru shoot rabbits at same location.

26 November   Cassidy and Albie Uluru shoot rabbits in vacant Crown Land north-east of Olgas.

30 November   Cassidy Uluru and Jacky Tjupuru shoot rabbits on Britten-Jones Creek, a short distance beyond the southern border of the Park.

7 December   Cassidy Uluru and Jacky Tjupuru shoot rabbits in the Olgas.

10 December   Paddy Uluru, his son Albie and Pompy Douglas shoot a perenti near Cave Hill (just across South Australian border).

11 December   Same men shoot two euro near Kulpitjata (in Petermann Reserve).

16 December   Jacky Tjupuru shoots two red kangaroo in Sedimentaries area of vacant Crown Land.

Fieldwork March to July 1978

25 March   Cassidy Uluru shoots two red kangaroo in Petermann Reserve, close to southern boundary of Park, on Britten-Jones Creek.

31 March   Toby Nangina, Peter Bulla, Paddy Uluru and Cassidy shoot two euro at Ilanula (west of Mount Conner, inside Curtin Springs Pastoral Lease).

1 April   Paddy Uluru seen in camp working on freshly collected mulga, manufacturing boomerangs.

4 April   Firewood collection in vacant Crown Land west of Ayers Rock.

5 April   Paddy Uluru and Cassidy shoot one red kangaroo on Britten-Jones Creek track.

9 April   Paddy Uluru collects wood to make heavy spears from Ayers Rock mulga in Park south of Olgas. Firewood collected at the same time.

16 April   Paddy Uluru collects wood from spear-bushes in Walpanya (Olgas) to make light spears. On return, picks 'native tobacco' from south face of Ayers Rock, which he gives to Napala Jack.

18 April   Jimmy Walkabout and Napala Jack collect firewood from south side of the Olgas.

19 April   Mary Captain and Lily Walkabout collect firewood next to road between Ayers Rock and the Olgas.

23 April   Paddy Uluru cuts mulga wood for boomerangs from grove adjacent to bed of Britten-Jones Creek, in Petermann Reserve south of Ayers Rock.

28 April   Jimmy Walkabout and Mary Captain collect firewood in Sedimentaries area of vacant Crown Land.

30 April   Dennis Matthews (Ranger) takes party of Aboriginal women to get bloodwood limbs for carving animals and coolamons from vacant Crown Land north-east of Olgas.

3 May   Paddy Uluru obtains quandong wood for boomerangs from vacant Crown Land north-west of Purrarra Well when on expedition to show me this site.

5 May   Pompy Wanampi shoots red kangaroo on Nulcharra Creek on the Yunanpanya estate while in the company of Pompy Douglas and Paddy Uluru. Kangaroo given to Paddy 'because Yunanpa is his country' (i.e. contains his birth site).

6 May   Jimmy and Lily Walkabout collect firewood in Park between Ayers Rock and the Olgas.

7 May   Jimmy and Lily collect chewing 'tobacco' from foot of south face of Ayers Rock.

15 May   Jimmy and Lily collect firewood from the Park on the south side of the Rock.

16 May   Paddy Uluru cuts lengths of spear-bush wood to make light spears.

At Docker River 19–30 May; no information on activities in claim area for this period.

15–22 June   Toby Nangina and his wife Ada camp on the north side of the Kelly Hills, close to the southern boundary of the vacant Crown Land.

16 June   Nipper Winmati and Paddy Uluru collect lengths of spear-bush wood from Walpanya, in the Olgas.

18–19 June   Mary Captain, Matjala and Lily Walkabout taken, at their request, to camp in the area of their own estates, near the head of Armstrong Creek. Here they collect wood for artefacts.

20 June   Paddy Uluru collects chewing 'tobacco' from Patji.

21 June   Paddy Uluru shoots two red kangaroo in vicinity of Patji and Tjapiya.

25 June   Pompy Douglas, Malcolm Winima, Tommy Minyinu and Paddy Uluru shoot two red kangaroo near Kulpitjata.

About one month after I left the field in 1978, Toby Nangina and Ada walked from Ayers Rock to Patji. Here Ada turned back, but Toby continued alone to Amata, on foot.

REFERENCES

GENERAL

Basedow, H. (1914), *Journal of the government north-west expedition*, Royal Geographical Society of Australasia, South Australian Branch, Adelaide.

Berndt, R.M. (1959), 'The Concept of the tribe in the Western Desert of Australia', *Oceania* **30**, 81–107.

———— (1970), *Australian Aboriginal Anthropology*, University of Western Australia Press, Nedlands.

———— (1972), 'The Walmadjeri and Gugadja', M.G. Bicchieri (ed.), op. cit., 177–216.

———— (1977) *Aborigines and Change: Australia in the 1970s*, Australian Institute of Aboriginal Studies, Canberra.

Bicchieri, M.G. (ed.) (1972), *Hunters and Gatherers Today*, Holt, Rinehart & Winston, New York.

Brokensha, P. (1975), *The Pitjantjatjara and their Crafts*, The Aboriginal Arts Board, Australia Council, Sydney.

Carruthers, J. (n.d.), Brief report on country triangulated in Everard, Musgrave, Mann and Tomkinson Ranges . . . 1888, 1889 and 1890, lodged in South Australian Archives, Adelaide.

Chippendale, G.M. (1963), 'Pasture degradation in central Australia, *Australian Journal of Agricultural Research*, **29**, 84–9.

Clune, F. (1942), *Last of the Australian Explorers*, Angus & Robertson, Sydney.

Coote, E. (1934), *Hell's Airport*, Petermann Press, Sydney.

Cutter, T. (1977), *Report on community health model: health by the people*, Central Australian Aboriginal Congress, Alice Springs.

Day, T.E. (1916), *Examination of the country west of the Overland Telegraph Line*, Northern Territory Bulletin No. 20, Department of Homes and Territories, Melbourne, (copy held in Australian Archives file CRS A3, item 22/2391).

Duguid, C. (1963), *No Dying Race*, Rigby, Adelaide.

———— (1972), *Doctor and the Aborigines*, Rigby, Adelaide.

Duncan, R. (1967), *The Northern Territory Pastoral Industry, 1863–1910*, Melbourne University Press, Melbourne.

Erskine, T.W. (1951), 'Land of no second chance', *Holiday and Travel*, August, 28–32, 40.

Finlayson, H.H. (1935), *The Red Centre*, Angus & Robertson, Sydney.

Foreman, D.J. (1965), *Explanatory Notes on the Ayers Rock Geological Map Sheet (1:250,000 series)*, Bureau of Mineral Resources, Canberra.

Fox, R.W. et al. (1977), *Ranger Uranium Environmental Inquiry Second Report*, Australian Government Publishing Service, Canberra.

Frith, H.J. (1973), *Wildlife Conservation*, Angus & Robertson, Sydney.

———— (1978). 'Wildlife resources in central Australia', in B.S. Hetzel, and H.J. Frith (eds) op.cit., 87–93.

Giles, W.E.P. (1889), *Australia Twice Traversed*, 2 vols, Sampson Low, London.

Gill, W. (1968), *Petermann Journey*, Rigby, Adelaide.

Gosse, W.C. (1874), *Report and diary of Mr W.C. Gosse's central and western exploring expedition, 1873*, South Australian Government Printer, Adelaide.

Gould, R.A. (n.d.), 'The Australian desert culture,' unpublished paper, prepared at University of Hawaii.

———— (1968), 'Living archaeology: the Ngatatjara of Western Australia', *Southwestern Journal of Anthropology* **24**, 101–22.

———— (1969a), 'Subsistence behaviour among the western desert Aboriginals of Australia'. *Oceania* **39**, 253–74.

———— (1969b), *Yiwara: foragers of the Australian desert*, Collins, London.

———— (1971), 'The Archaeologist as ethnographer: a case from the western desert of Australia', *World Archaeology* **3**, 143–77.

Gould, R.A. and C.S. Fowler (1972), 'Diggers and doggers: parallel failures in acculturation', *Southwestern Journal of Anthropology* **28**, 265–81.

Groom, A. (1950), *I Saw a Strange Land*, Angus and Robertson, Sydney.

Harney, W.E. (1968), *The Significance of Ayers Rock for Aborigines*. Northern Territory Reserves Board, Alice Springs.

———— (1969), *To Ayers Rock and Beyond*, 2nd edn (1st edn 1963), Rigby, Adelaide.

Hartwig, M.C. (1965), *The Progress of White Settlement in the Alice Springs District and its effect upon the Aboriginal inhabitants, 1860–1894*, unpublished PhD thesis, University of South Australia, Adelaide.

REFERENCES

Hagen, R. and M. Rowell (1978), *A claim to areas of traditional land by the Alyawarra and Kaititja*, Central Land Council, Alice Springs.

Hayden, B. (1979), *Palaeolithic reflections: lithic technology and ethnographic excavations among Australian Aborigines*, Australian Institute of Aboriginal Studies, Canberra.

Hetzel, B.S. and H.J. Frith (eds.) (1978), *The Nutrition of Aborigines in relation to the ecosystem of central Australia*, Commonwealth Scientific and Industrial Research Organisation, Melbourne.

Hiatt, L.R. (1962), 'Local organisation among the Australian Aborigines', *Oceania* **32**, 267–86.

Hilliard, W.M. (1968), *The People in between: the Pitjantjatjara people of Ernabella*, Hodder and Stoughton, London.

Idriess, I. (1931), *Lasseter's Last Ride*, Angus and Robertson, Sydney.

Isaacs, J. (1980), *Australian dreaming: 40,000 years of Aboriginal History*, Lansdowne Press, Sydney.

Jenkins, H.A. et al. (1973), *House of Representatives Standing Committee on Environment and Conservation report on Ayers Rock–Mount Olga National Park*. Parliament of the Commonwealth of Australia, Parliamentary Paper No. 215 of 1973.

Latz, P. (1978), 'Changes in Aboriginal land management in relation to fire and food plants in Central Australia', in B.S. Hetzel and H.J. Frith (eds) op. cit., 77–85.

Layton, R. and M. Rowell (1979), *Ayers Rock–Mount Olga National Park and Lake Amadeus traditional land claim: claim book*, Central Land Council, Alice Springs.

Layton, R. (1983a), 'Ambilineal descent and Pitjantjatjara rights to land', N. Peterson and M. Langton, (eds) op. cit., 15–32.

———(1983b), 'Pitjantjatjara processes and the structure of the Land Rights Act', in N. Peterson and M. Langton (eds) op. cit., 226–37.

Lewis, D. (1976), 'Observations on route-finding and spatial orientation ... (in) central Australia'. *Oceania* **46**, 249–82.

Long, J. (1963), 'Preliminary work in planning welfare development in the Petermann Ranges', *Australian Territories* **3** (2), 4–12.

Love, J.R.B. and L. Balfour (1937), *Ernabella Mission Report*, Board of Missions of Presbyterian Church of Australia, Adelaide (?) (copy held in Australian Archives file A659, item 41/1/221.

Macfarlane, W.V. (1978), 'Aboriginal desert hunter/gatherers in transition', in B.S. Hetzel and H.J. Frith (eds) op. cit., 49–62.

Mackay, D. (1929), 'The Mackay exploring expedition, central Australia', *Geographical Journal* **73**, 258–64.

——— (1930), *Report of Mackay Aerial Survey expedition, Central Australia, May–June 1930*, in Mackay Expedition Aerial Survey of Central Australia, Australian Archives CRS A431; 47/1640, June 1927–July 1947.

——— (1943), *Central Australia: the opinion of a pastoralist*, in Mackay Expedition Aerial Survey of Central Australia, Australian Archives CRS A431; 47/1640, June 1927–July 1947.

Meggitt, M.J. (1962), *Desert People*, Chicago University Press, Chicago.

Milliken, E.P. (1971), 'History of the Welfare Branch in the Northern Territory', in C.A. Gibb, et al., *The Report of the Committee to review the situation of Aborigines on pastoral properties in the Northern Territory* (The Gibb Report), Australian Government Publishing Service, Canberra, 89–93.

Mountford, C.P. (1950), *Brown Men and Red Sand*, Angus & Robertson, Sydney.

——— (1977), *Ayers Rock: its people, their beliefs and their art*, 2nd edn, (1st edn, 1965), Rigby, Adelaide.

Munn, N.D. (1965), *A Report on field research at Areyonga*, unpublished report held by Australian Institute of Aboriginal Studies, AIAS Document No. 65/280.

——— *(1973)*, *Walpiri Iconography*, Cornell University Press, Ithaca.

Myers, F.R. (1976), *To Have and to Hold: a study of persistence and change in Pintubi social life*, unpublished PhD thesis, Bryn Mawr, Philadelphia.

O'Connell, J.F. (1976), *Report on investigations of Alyawara land claims*, unpublished paper prepared at Department of Prehistory, Research School of Pacific Studies, Australian National University, Canberra.

Ovington, J.D. (1980), *Kakadu National Park: Plan of Management*. Australian National Parks and Wildlife Service, Canberra.

Peterson, N. (ed.) (1976), *Tribes and Boundaries in Australia*, Australian Institute of Aboriginal Studies, Canberra.

———— (1978), 'The traditional pattern of subsistence to 1975', in B.S. Hetzel and H.J. Frith (eds), op. cit., 25–35.

———— R. Hagen and M. Rowell (1978), *A Claim to areas of traditional land by the Warlpiri, and Kartangarurru-Kurintji*, 3rd edn, Central Land Council, Alice Springs.

———— and M. Langton (eds) (1983), *Aborigines, Land and Landrights*, Australian Institute of Aboriginal Studies, Canberra.

Roff, D. (1976), *Mammals of the Ayers Rock-Mt Olga National Park*, Northern Territory Reserves Board, Alice Springs.

Rose, F.G.G. (1965), *The Wind of Change in Central Australia*, Akademie Verlag, Berlin.

Silberbauer, G.B. (1971), 'Ecology of the Ernabella Aboriginal Community', *Anthropological Forum* **3**, 21–36.

Spencer, W.B. (1919), *Professor W. Baldwin Spencer's Report re. N.T. Natives*, Northern Territory Bulletin No. 7, Department of Homes and Territories, Melbourne (copy held in Australian Archives file CRS A3 item 19/2897).

———— and F.J. Gillen (1912), *Across Australia*, Macmillan, London.

Stanner, W.E.H. (1965), 'Aboriginal territorial organisation', *Oceania* **36**, 1–26.

Strehlow, T.G.H. (1965), 'Culture, social structure and environment in Central Australia', in R.M. Berndt (ed.) *Aboriginal Man in Australia*, Angus & Robertson, Sydney, 121–45.

———— (1969a), *Journey to Horseshoe Bend*, Angus & Robertson, Sydney.

———— (1969b), 'Mythology of the Centralian Aborigine' (part one), *Inland Review* June/August, Alice Springs, 11–17.

———— (1970), 'Geography and the totemic landscape in central Australia', in R.M. Berndt (ed.) op. cit., 92–140.

———— (1971), *Songs of Central Australia*, Angus & Robertson, Sydney.

Terry, M. (n.d.), *Untold Miles* Selwyn, London.

Tietkins, W.H. (1891), *Journal of the Central Australian Exploring Expedition*, South Australian Government Printer, Adelaide.

Tindale, N.B. (1959), 'Totemic beliefs in the western desert of Australia', *Records of the South Australian Museum* **13**, 305–32.

———— (1972), 'The Pitjantjatjara', in M.G. Bicchieri (ed.) op. cit., 217–67.

———— (1974), *Aboriginal Tribes of Australia*, Australian National University Press, Canberra.

Tonkinson, R. (1978), *The Mardudjara Aborigines: living the dream in Australia's desert*, Holt, Rinehart & Winston, New York.

Toohey, J. (1979a), *Land claim by Warlpiri and Kartangarurru-Kurintji: report by the Aboriginal Land Commissioner . . .*, Australian Government Publishing Service, Canberra.

———— (1979b), *Land Claim by Alyawarra and Kaititja: report by the Aboriginal Land Commissioner . . .*, Australian Government Publishing Services, Canberra.

————(1980), *Uluru (Ayers Rock) National Park and Lake Amadeus/ Luritja Land Claim: report by the Aboriginal Land Commissioner . . .*, Australian Government Publishing Service, Canberra.

Wallace, N. (1977), 'Change in spiritual and ritual life in Pitjantjatjara society, 1966 to 1973', in R.M. Berndt (ed.) op. cit., 74–89.

Wallace, P. and N. Wallace (1977), *Killing Me Softly*, Nelson, Melbourne.

Woenne, S. (1977), 'Old country, new territory: some implications of the settlement process', in R.M. Berndt (ed.) op. cit., 54–64.

Woodward, A.E. (1973), *Aboriginal Land Rights Commission, first report*. Parliamentary Paper No. 138 of 1973, Australian Government Publishing Service, Canberra.

Yengoyan, A.A. (1970), 'Demographic factors in Pitjandjara social organisation', in R.M. Berndt (ed.) op. cit., 79–91.

Material from the Australian Archives
(bracketed codes refer to references in text)

(AA1) *AA:CRS A659; 40/1/1428* 'Suggestions re Aboriginal Reserves in south-west of Northern Territory, January

1935–May 1940'. Letter from Association for Protection of Native Races to Minister for Interior; quoting Albrecht, and letter from Albrecht to Deputy Administrator, Alice Springs.

(AA2)   *AA:CRS A659; 41/1/101*   'Death of Native Lallilicki at Mount Cavanagh Station, trial of H.J. Kitto and P. Deconlay, February 1941–May 1943'.

(AA3)   *AA:CRS A3; NT 14/7104*   'Aboriginal Reserve, Musgrave, Mann and Tomkinson Ranges 1873–1919'.

(AA4)   *AA:CRS A659; 40/1/1428*   'Suggestions re Aboriginal Reserves in south-west of Northern Territory, January 1935–May 1940'. Strehlow proposals summarised by Cook, Chief Protector of Aborigines.

(AA5)   *AA:CRS A659; 40/1/1428*   'Suggestions re Aboriginal Reserves in south-west of Northern Territory, January 1935–May 1940'. Memo from Carrodus 29 April, 1937.

(AA6)   *AA:CRS A659; 40/1/1428*   'Suggestions re Aboriginal Reserves in south-west of Northern Territory, January 1935–May 1940. Memo of 16/12/39.

(AA7)   *AA:CRS A659; 41/1/221*   'Ernabella Mission, N.T. Report by Rev J.R.B. Love and Dr L. Balfour, March 1937–July 1942'. Letter from Duguid, April 13, 1940.

(AA8)   *AA:CRS A659; 40/1/1428*   'Suggestions re Aboriginal Reserves in south-west of Northern Territory, January 1935–May 1940'.

(AA9)   *AA:CRS F1; 52/470*   'Office of the Administrator (Northern Territory). Correspondence files, annual single number series, South West Reserve, November 1940–1952'.

(AA10)   *AA:CRS F1; 52/1077*   'Proposed Airstrip Ayers Rock, March 1952–1957'. H. Barclay to the Administrator, 23 February 1954.

(AA11)   *AA:CRS F1; 52/470*   'Office of the Administrator (Northern Territory). Correspondence files, annual single number series, South West Reserve, November 1940–1952'. G. Sweeney to Director of Native Affairs, 14 October 1947.

(AA12)   *AA:CRS F1; 52/1077*   'Proposed Airstrip Ayers Rock, March 1952–1957'. Letter 1 July 1953.

(AA13)   *AA:CRS F1; 52/1077*   'Proposed Airstrip Ayers Rock, March 1952–1957'. Letter from R.G. Hill to Minister for Territories, 19 June 1953.

(AA14)   *AA:CRS F1; 51/799*   'Native School at Areyonga and Teachers Residence, February 1951–1954'. Letter of 2 July 1953.

(AA15)   *AA:CRS A659; 41/1/221*   'Ernabella Mission, Northern Territory Report by Rev J.R.B. Love and Dr L. Balfour, March 1937–July 1942'.

(AA16)   *AA:CRS A659; 41/1/221*   'Ernabella Mission, Northern Territory Report by Rev J.R.B. Love and Dr L. Balfour, March 1937–July 1942. J.A. Carrodus letter of 18 May 1937.

(AA17)   *AA:CRS F1; 52/1077*   'Proposed Airstrip Ayers Rock, March 1952–1957'. Letter to Secretary, Department of Territories, 28 July 1953.

(AA18)   *AA:CRS F1; 51/799*   'Native School at Areyonga and Teachers Residence, February 1951–1954'. Letter to Senior Education Officer, 2 July 1953.

(AA19)   *AA: CA855 E72; DL807*   'The King against Numberlin and Nangee'.

(AA20)   *AA: CA855 E72; DL444*   'Inquest: Kai Umen (Aboriginal) held at Alice Springs 17 January 1935'.

(AA21)   *AA: CA855 E72; DL807*   'The King against Numberlin and Nangee'.

Welfare Branch correspondence and reports

(WB1)   *64/44/11*   Assistant Director Welfare Branch, Northern Territory Administration, Alice Springs, letter of 16 July 1964.

(WB2)   *64/44/31*   Patrol Officer D.A. Stewart, report on itinerant Aboriginals: south-west area, to District Welfare Officer, Alice Springs, dated 28 October 1965.

(WB3)   *65/379*   Director of Social Welfare Branch, Darwin, letter of 20 July 1965.

(WB4)   *64/44/33*   District Welfare Officer, report to Assistant Director (Southern), Welfare Branch, dated 3 November 1965.

(WB5)   *64/44/38*   Patrol Officer D.A. Stewart, report on itinerant Aborigines, south-west area, to District Welfare Officer, dated 18 July 1966.

INDEX

Administration

3rd edition

NVQ LEVEL 1

Carol Carysforth
Mike Neild

Student handbook

Heinemann

Heinemann Educational Publishers,
Halley Court, Jordan Hill, Oxford OX2 8EJ
A division of Reed Educational & Professional Publishing Ltd

Heinemann is a registered trademark of
Reed Educational & Professional Publishing Limited

OXFORD MELBOURNE AUCKLAND
JOHANNESBURG BLANTYRE GABORONE
IBADAN PORTSMOUTH NH (USA) CHICAGO

© Carol Carysforth, Mike Neild 2002

First published 2002
2006 2005 2004 2003 2002
10 9 8 7 6 5 4 3 2 1

A catalogue record for this book is available from
the British Library on request.

ISBN 0 435 45168 5

Typeset by ⫪ Tek-Art, Croydon, Surrey

Printed and bound in Great Britain by The Bath Press Ltd, Bath

Tel: 01865 888058 www.heinemann.co.uk

Contents

SPECIAL NOTE

Guidance on the following skills is freely available on the Heinemann
website at www.heinemann.co.uk/vocational/NVQ password
ADMINSKILLS): Improving your writing skills; Improving your number
skills; Your rights and responsibilities at work.

Council for Administration

This NVQ/SVQ publication is based on the national occupational standards developed by the Council for Administration (CfA), which is the Government-approved body representing the sector of Administration. Copyright of the national occupational standards is the property of the CfA and, as such, the standards may not be reproduced or transmitted in any form or by any means without written permission from the CfA.

For further information on the work of the CfA, including the Administration Standards, please contact:

The CfA
18/20 Bromell's Road
London SW4 0BG
Telephone: 020 7627 9876
Fax: 020 7627 9877
Email: **nto@cfa.uk.com**
Website: **www.cfa.uk.com**